FIGHTIN
BODY POLLUTION

STAYING HEALTHY IN AN UNHEALTHY WORLD

Manjul Publishing House

First published in India by

Manjul Publishing House Pvt. Ltd.
Corporate Office: 2nd Floor, Usha Preet Complex,
42 Malviya Nagar, Bhopal, INDIA-462 003
E-mail: manjul@manjulindia.com Website: www.manjulindia.com
Registered Office: 10 Nishat Colony, Bhopal, INDIA-462 003

Distributed in India by
book supply co

First published in India 2007
Third impression 2010

ISBN   978-81-8322-110-8

Printed & bound in India by Manipal Press Limited

Table of Contents

Foreword 1

Introduction 3

Chapter 1 - What is Body Pollution? 5

Chapter 2 - How Does Body Pollution Affect You? 13

Chapter 3 - Fighting Back with Good Nutrition 23

Chapter 4 - Vitamins: What's in a Name? 35

Chapter 5 - Minerals: Salt of the Earth 49

Chapter 6 - The Healing Power of Herbs 61

Chapter 7 - The Phenomenal Power of Phytonutrients 73

Chapter 8 - The Marvelous Benefits of Fibre 85

Chapter 9 - Obesity: A Global Epidemic 93

Chapter 10 - Staying Young at Any Age 107

Chapter 11 - Stress and Exercise 121

Chapter 12 - Now for a Brand New Life 135

References 141

Index 147

Foreword

As a cardiologist practicing in a busy community hospital, I meet on a daily basis with patients who suffer from cardiovascular disease. Cardiovascular disease accounts for the death of more people than any other disease. Of those deaths, at least half are due specifically to coronary artery disease, that is, clogging of the arteries supplying blood to the heart muscle.

As the baby boomer population ages, we will see more and more cardiac disease in the future. Although some patients may suffer from cardiovascular disease due to genetic and pre-determined factors, many patients' conditions are affected by environmental factors.

We live in a rapidly changing environment which can be detrimental to our health. With busy careers and time constraints, many people do not have the time to eat a proper diet or to exercise effectively - poor nutrition and lack of exercise play a significant role in many cases of cardiovascular disease.

In addition, our increasingly polluted environment can have a measurable negative effect on health. A recent study from Harvard Medical School suggested that smog may increase the risk of myocardial infarction (heart attack) by up to 50%. Many people do not realize the indisputable link between the environment we live in and many of the diseases that are most prevalent today.

Many of the risk factors for cardiac disease including hypertension (high blood pressure), hyperlipidemia (high cholesterol levels), obesity and diabetes are strongly linked to poor nutrition. Proper nutritional intake is essential to prevent or control many of these conditions. Unfortunately, with busy lifestyles, many patients' dietary intake is high in fat and void of nutrition including essential minerals and vitamins as well as fibre.

As you will see in the following pages, many people find it quite difficult to fulfill their dietary requirements even when eating what they think is a "well-balanced diet" and for many people, nutritional supplements are an effective method of restoring those missing essential nutrients. On a similar note, due to the over processed nature of many of our foods, most patients do not take in enough dietary fibre. Increasing fiber intake can improve cardiac heath (by lowering cholesterol levels and controlling blood sugar levels), and may be beneficial in controlling or preventing other diseases such as bowel problems.

In addition to proper nutrition, exercise remains a mainstay of cardiac prevention. Increasing exercise will help to prevent or control heart disease, diabetes, hypertension, osteoporosis, depression and obesity to name just a few. I find that very few of my patients perform the recommended 30 to 60 minutes of moderate exercise, most days of the week.

Although I see many patients in my practice with advanced cardiac disease, I see many more patients with more minor forms of disease as well as people who are currently free of disease and who want to prevent or delay the onset of problems in the future. They want to ensure that they have made every lifestyle change possible to protect their health. They are looking for a well-rounded approach to improving their nutrition, eliminating their exposure to pollution and increasing their activity level, with a view towards health promotion and prevention of disease. Although everyone recognizes the importance of modern medicine in the treatment of disease, I think that a book such as this is an essential guide to help people develop daily habits to protect their health.

Paul M. Hacker, M.D., FRCPC, FACC

Introduction

It seems that not a day goes by without seeing some negative story in the newspaper or on television regarding our environment. Global warming, air and water pollution, the thinning ozone layer…the list goes on. As a nutritionist, I can't help wondering what this is doing to our health. How could environmental pollution damage the earth without damaging us as well? The effect of the environment on our health really hit me on a trip to Asia when I noticed more than half the people walking or cycling the streets wearing face masks to protect themselves from dirty air. Thankfully I live in Canada, I thought. Then I learned that air pollution can travel from Asia to North America in 3 days - not much longer than it took me to fly home!

The truth is that every living thing on the planet is affected by the environment, and none more than we are. How can we protect ourselves from the damage of environmental pollution that enters our bodies - what I call body pollution? What steps can we take to maintain or improve our health in today's polluted world?

This book is your guide to using the latest research into the benefits of nutrition, food supplements, exercise, and stress reduction to maximize your health. Although we cannot avoid pollution entirely, we can all take steps to reduce its negative impact on our body. I outline easy and practical steps you can take today, that over time, will add years of productive, healthy time to your life.

Better health is a learning process and you may find that Chapters One and Two contain some pretty shocking information about the environment we live in and what it's doing to our health. I urge you to keep reading - it's important to be aware of what's happening with our environment and how it affects our health. Why should information that is vital to your health only be known to scientists?

Starting with Chapter Three, you'll learn how to fight body pollution and optimize your health using all the tools available to us. You'll read about the most up to date research on vitamins, minerals, herbs, phytonutrients and diet. This information will show you how to maintain your present good health, or rebuild your health to the highest level possible. Fighting body pollution means having vibrant energy, staying young and vital longer and, as a bonus, looking good. In short, fighting body pollution means achieving the best health possible for you and your family.

To help you learn and apply the information in this book, I've provided some extras to make it easier:

 Fast Facts - relevant facts regarding our environment and our health that may surprise or shock you

 Did You Know? - interesting information that may counter or dispel things you thought were true

 Health Tip - practical tips you can apply to your daily routine to improve your health

 Take Action Today - each chapter ends with steps for you to take that will help you fight body pollution and transform your health

Now it's up to you. Apply the ideas and principles in this book and you're on your way to Fighting Body Pollution and staying healthy in an unhealthy world. The payoff will be better health, vitality and a long productive life.

To your good health!

Paul Kramer, R.N.C

CHAPTER

What is Body Pollution?

Did You Know...

Only 5% of pesticides reach target weeds and the rest runs off into water and goes into the air we breathe.

Let's do a little time travel - back millions of years to the dawn of intelligent life on this beautiful planet. See how pristine and unspoiled the world is. Notice the untouched environment and the bountiful earth. Take a deep breath of wonderful pure, clean air as you look around you. Can you believe the beauty?

Nothing is artificial or unnatural, and the environment has the ability to sustain itself. People drink clean water from natural sources and diets consist mainly of uncultivated fruits, vegetables and lean meats.

There are no plastics, food additives or chemical sprays and no cars or factories to pollute the air. Asthma, heart disease, diabetes and cancer are unheard of because they simply don't exist. These modern-day chronic illnesses are the high price we pay for the conveniences of modern life.

Okay, now let's return to the present and look at our world as though we were travelers from ancient times. Suddenly, it's difficult to breathe. Smog-filled cities choke us and our lakes are too polluted to swim in. Drinking untreated water is unthinkable. We don't recognize the 'foods' which are highly refined with added colours and preservatives that many people are eating. The diet seems to consist mostly of saturated fats, salt and/or sugar with a shortage of fresh fruits and vegetables.

Health Tip

Indoor air pollution can be worse than outdoors. To reduce indoor air pollution levels in your home, open windows regularly.

Fast Fact

Millions of people around the world have no choice but to consume water that exceeds the lead contamination level deemed acceptable by the World Health Organization.

We see people eating a large meal of fatty foods and then spending the evening in front of the television set as their children play video games on the computer. The next day, the kids are driven to school as the parents go to work which means sitting in front of the computer once again. Although people aren't exercising much, they seem chronically tired.

Shocking, isn't it? It leaves you wondering about the intelligence of a species that damages its own environment. There's no doubt that our ancient ancestors would be really confused by our behavior.

Although the first environmental damage likely came from hunters who burned down forests in order to scare the animals out, we can trace the beginnings of irreversible and sustained ecological damage directly back to the Industrial Revolution some 250 years ago, and all the trappings that came along with it.

Since then, there's been a race to 'succeed' with little thought to the damage we're doing along the way. For centuries we got away with this short-sighted view. As long as there was still plenty of forest and farmland and the water was more or less clean, we didn't worry.

Fast Fact

One billion people, mostly women and children, are regularly exposed to levels of indoor air pollution exceeding World Health Organization guidelines by up to 100 times.

It's time we did. Think about it. For roughly two million years, human beings lived essentially the same way with the same basic requirements to sustain life. In the very small space of only 250 years, we've undergone massive lifestyle changes in terms of what we eat, drink and do in our spare time. Yet somehow we expect that our bodies will magically adapt to all these changes.

Not without protesting! And the protest can take the form of asthma, heart disease, cancer, etc. All of these diseases are on the rise; even diseases we thought were conquered are making a chilling comeback. Think of illness as your body's way of protesting the artificial modern lifestyle.

Culturally, you're very different from your ancestors, the hunter-gatherers. Yet genetically and physically, you haven't changed. Your genetic structure, which controls every function of your body, is essentially the same as those who lived eons before you. Nourish these genes well and they'll keep you healthy. Give these genes artificial foods or expose them to environmental toxins and they go awry. That could mean aging faster or developing a chronic illness.

Since we eat, breathe and live in this modern environment, ingesting these toxins is inevitable. Many of these pollutants end up being stored in our bodies. I think of this buildup of contaminants as "body pollution". Our bodies were simply never designed to metabolize and digest these modern adulterated foods and our systems struggle to detoxify such overwhelming amounts of pollution.

Here's how body pollution works. Once a foreign substance enters the body, it has to be detoxified and made water soluble so that it can be safely eliminated. The liver and the kidneys are the main organs responsible for detoxification while the lungs, skin and intestines also play an important role. But even with all these powerful allies on our side, our bodies simply can't detoxify and eliminate all the chemicals we ingest. It does its best but we're still left with a damaging residue.

When the main organs have more toxins than they can handle, the still active or partially deactivated chemicals are stored in the fatty tissues - possibly even in the brain and central nervous system. Slowly, these reactive and toxic compounds can be released into the bloodstream, disrupting the systems of the body and causing premature aging and disease.

So this is what we call progress! Overloading our bodies with unnatural and harmful substances. It's a step forward all right - a step forward into premature aging and chronic illness.

While we're well aware of the damage that pollutants can cause to the environment in terms of global warming or chemical spills, somehow we don't make the leap in logic when it comes to our own buildup of body pollution. Most of us know that carbon monoxide emissions damage the trees and stunt their growth but rarely do we realize that all this pollution is also doing internal damage to us.

Did You Know...

Roughly four hundred million tons of chemicals are used or produced worldwide each year.

Did You Know...

Alternative trans-
portation policies
initiated during
the 1996 summer
Olympics in
Atlanta not only
reduced vehicle
exhaust and air
pollutants such as
ozone by about
30%, they also
decreased the
number of acute
asthma attacks by
40% and pedi-
atric emergency
admissions by
about 19%

It shows in how much energy we have, in our outlook on life, in our capacity for enjoyment. It shows in terms of how well we feel and how well we actually are. We've come to think it's normal to feel exhausted after a full work day since we don't know any other way of living.

The Air We Breathe

Thankfully, there is another way and I'm going to reveal it to you as you read on. First, I'm going to ask you to do a little research of your own. Next time you are dropping your children or grandchildren off at school, see how many kids have inhalers to help them with asthma-related breathing problems. Then think back to when you attended school and the magnitude of the problem will hit you. The level of pollution has overwhelmed children's natural ability to fight back and deactivate the toxic overload. In certain countries, 30-40% of asthma cases and 20-30% of all respiratory diseases can be directly linked to air pollution.

The Water We Drink

For a good barometer of the quality of our current water supply, we need to look at the effect pollution is having on marine life. A dead orca whale recently found off the Washington coast appears to be the most toxic mammal ever tested (so far) with levels of polychlorinated biphenyls (PCB's) so great that the assessment machines had to be reset in order to be able to measure the levels.

Fast Fact

Studies show that over 80% of U.S. streams and rivers are contaminated with a broad array of medical drugs, including hormones, antibiotics, antidepressants and heart medications, as well as chemicals from personal care and household cleaning products.

The sad fact is that whales in the Canadian Gulf of St. Lawrence (and in many other parts of the world) are so full of PCB's that they qualify as toxic dumpsites under US environmental laws.

The Food We Eat

So much for our water. Now think about the food you eat and the fact that over 10,000 food chemicals and additives are currently in use in your food supply.

All of these chemicals are used to make processed and packaged food look and taste better and, of course, last as long as possible on the store shelves. Many of the chemicals end up being stored in your body.

Food chemistry became an essential science as society developed and people began to move from the rural areas to the cities. Food had to be distributed over longer and longer distances before reaching the consumer so somehow it needed to be preserved.

Fast Fact

The average person consumes over fourteen pounds of food chemicals and additives each year. That means that over the course of a normal lifespan, we consume more than one thousand pounds of food chemicals and additives, not including those found in water and air.

Health Tip

Using only organic based cleaners in your home can reduce your exposure to chemicals considerably.

Those lovely looking apples in your neighborhood shop were most likely grown thousands of miles away, picked while they were still green and exposed to ethylene gas so they could ripen as they were being shipped to their destination in a truck. Not only do these fruits still carry a residue of the chemical but because they were picked early, they may have little or no nutritional value by the time they reach your kitchen table.

Our modern food supply has become a mixture of chemicals and additives with the emphasis on appearance and taste as well as shelf life, rather than on the nutritional value. The food industry is being driven by people's reliance on convenience foods that fit in with busy lifestyles. The invention of the TV dinner, fast food restaurant drive-through, pre-packaged ready-to-serve foods and super-sized meals have all contributed to more calories and more chemicals with fewer essential nutrients.

Body Pollution Affects Every One of Us

After doing your research, if you're still not convinced that modern society is not conducive to a healthy lifestyle - consider this:

Back in 1976, the U. S. Environmental Protection Agency began a program of collecting and analyzing human fat tissue samples - looking for toxic compounds. They searched for and studied 54 different environmental toxins. What they found was alarming. 100% of the people they studied had toxic chemicals stored in their bodies and at least 76% of all people had more than 20 different chemicals stored. Think about it! Every single person had some toxins in their bodies - undeniable proof that body pollution is a very real concept and a threat to your health.

Health Tip

Thoroughly washing fruits and vegetables with a non toxic detergent will remove many of the chemicals. If available, try special fruit and vegetable washes.

Fast Fact

Out of 2700 chemicals that are marketed in quantities above 1000 tons per year, there is insufficient or no basic toxicity data on 86% of them.

While you may not be able to pronounce some of the chemicals you see in the following table, I am certain that you will be very familiar with their sources.

Table 1-1: US EPA Analysis of Toxins in Human Fat Tissue Samples

Compound	Possible Common Source	% people containing toxins in fat tissue
Styrene	styrene based cups	100%
1, 4-Dichlorobenzene	house deodorizers, mothballs	100%
Xylene	gasoline, paints, lacquers	100%
Ethylphenol OCDD	drinking water, herbicides, wood treatments, auto exhausts, incinerators	100%
1,2,3,4,5,6,7,8 HpCDD	wood treatments, auto exhaust, herbicides, incinerators	89%
HxCDD	gasoline	96%
Benzene	drinking water	96%
Chlorobenzene	gasoline, produce	96%
Ethylbenzene p, pl-DDE 1, 2, 3, 4, 5, 6, 7, 8, HpCDF	wood treatments, auto exhaust, herbicides	93%

Let's look at another famous study of particular interest. It took place in Biosphere 2 which was intended to be a self-contained, self-sustaining greenhouse and colony in the Arizona desert. This was as pristine an environment as humanly possibly in today's polluted world - almost mimicking how we used to live.

Participants followed a low calorie, nutrient dense natural diet, drank pure water and breathed clean air - in other words, they lived in an environment free of body pollution.

Results of this study were both revealing and provocative. Over the two year study, participants demonstrated substantial weight loss, a remarkable fall in blood cholesterol, blood pressure and fasting glucose. In other words, they became healthy again.

Even more amazing is that when their blood was measured for common insecticides and pollutants such as DDE and PCB's, researchers found levels of these fat soluble toxicants initially increased and then decreased.

What does this mean? Well, as I mentioned, toxins are stored in fat tissues. So, as these people burned fat and lost weight, toxins stored in this body fat were released causing blood levels to initially rise. It's a process many natural health care practitioners call cleansing and it happens as your body begins to get healthier and sloughs off poisons. As the body was able to clear and excrete these pollutants, blood levels fell dramatically - proving once again the fact that body pollution exists in every one of us.

Did You Know...

Researchers find extremely high levels of mercury contamination in all samples of processed foods made in Japan from dolphin entrails such as liver, kidneys and lungs.

Conclusion

Our world is vastly different from that of our ancestors. While we're more aware of environmental pollution today than ever before, we can't avoid it. We eat, breathe and live in our modern environment, making the ingestion of toxins a part of everyday life. The US EPA experiments and Biosphere 2 are our proof that clearly there is no escape. Body pollution affects each and every one of us. There's absolutely no doubt that we all carry toxic compounds in our bodies. The question is exactly how much and how do they affect our health?

Did You Know...

The U.S. FDA did a survey looking at several food chemicals and found an alarming amount of pesticide residues in certain foods. DDE was found in 100% of samples of raisins, spinach, chile con carne and beef. 93% of processed cheese, hamburger, hot dogs, bologna, collards, chicken, turkey and ice cream sandwiches also contained DDE.

Take Action Today

1. *Reduce your use of chemicals around the home - common sources include lawn and garden chemicals and home cleaning products.*

2. *Be a responsible car owner and leave your car at home when you can. Look into alternative means of transportation.*

3. *Do your part in protecting the environment by recycling as much as possible.*

CHAPTER

How Does Body Pollution Affect You?

Coal mines have always been dangerous places. Before modern technology was available, one way of testing whether the mine was safe was for one miner to go in ahead of the others, carrying a canary in a cage. If the mine was emitting toxic gases, the canary would become sick or die - serving as a warning to the miners.

I think of that canary when I hear of whales that lose their navigational abilities and wash up on shores because they're so polluted or when I read about PCB exposed marine life with both male and female sexual characteristics. I'm further reminded when I read that the number of childhood leukemia cases is on the rise along with many other diseases. These days, there are a lot of 'canaries' serving as our warning.

I'm also hoping that you get the message because it's a very powerful one. The first step toward making a change is to become informed. That's often difficult when the information is alarming. It's worthwhile though, because once you're informed, you'll have a lot more control over your health and your family's health. Think about it - the animals and marine life that we're polluting have no say in the matter. They don't get a vote. You do, so why not use your information to your advantage?

How Body Pollution Affects Your Health

Still with me? Great! We know that, wherever we live, we have inherited a toxic environment that leaves us with a burden of body pollution. Think of body pollu-

Health Tip

The herb dandelion can help detoxify and cleanse your liver - one of the main organs needed to rid the body of toxins.

tion as a toxic waste dump that your vital organs do their best to cope with. These foreign chemicals that you take into your body need to be deactivated. While your body has the ability to detoxify, often it becomes overloaded and becomes less and less able to deal with body pollution. This can create permanent organ damage and also produce harmful by-products which remain active and stored in your body tissues (Look at our EPA chart to refresh your memory).

Every living creature has measurable levels of toxic chemicals stored in the body which when released can cause cellular damage. This damage may result in organ damage, a weakened immune system, and more susceptibility to disease. At best, these stored toxins place your body under incredible stress. You simply were never intended to handle the massive load that you ingest on a daily basis. It's like walking around a landmine - sooner or later, you're bound to trip over it! No wonder you feel tired for no apparent reason...your body is working hard to clean out toxins. If it is overwhelmed for a long stretch of time, sooner or later, you'll get sick.

Fast Fact

Doctors of environmental medicine estimate that 25% to 50% of the current population suffers from some sort of environmental related illness.

Free Radicals

Free radicals are one of the most destructive by-products of body pollution. They are produced naturally by the body in small amounts, but become a problem when too many are created as a result of body pollution overload.

Think of free radicals as your body's rebel molecules - they're highly reactive and have only one electron instead of the usual pair. In a battle for survival, they search out healthy cells in your body and steal the extra electron they need. These little thieves end up permanently damaging healthy cells. When you produce a large number of free radicals, a chain reaction occurs, causing even more to be produced. It's a vicious cycle.

Just as a car rusts from oxidation, your body 'rusts' from the oxidizing effects of free radicals. And the same way that a few spots of rust on your car eventually turns into a gaping hole, the 'rust' that free radicals create over time degrades your body's systems which makes you much more open to infections and illness.

Free radicals may be a culprit in many illnesses such as cancer, arthritis, diabetes, cataracts and heart disease and there's much evidence that they not only contribute to disease but accelerate the aging process as well.

Many sources of body pollution cause the production of free radicals. Every time you take a breath, you take in hundreds of chemicals from things such as air fresheners used in your home, auto exhaust, cigarette smoke and industrial emissions - all of these result in the creation of free radicals. Every time you eat, free radicals are made by the body in response to pesticides and food chemicals. Chlorine and heavy metals such as mercury, lead and cadmium often found in many sources of drinking water can also result in the production of free radicals.

Health Tip

Drinking only bottled, purified or distilled water will dramatically reduce your intake of chemicals and heavy metals.

Fast Fact

Air pollution is predicted to cause 8 million deaths annually by the year 2020.

This overload of free radicals is only one of the ways body pollution contributes to the decline of our health. Constant contamination from your environment has a negative impact on every part of your body and every aspect of your health. It's not surprising that old diseases are making a comeback and the ones that have been with us for a long time continue to be on the rise. Not to mention the new diseases we are faced with. Only in the last fifty years have we been forced to cope with the half-million or so synthetic chemicals floating around in the atmosphere.

Immune System

The body's immune system can't possibly operate effectively under this strain. It wasn't until AIDS (Acquired Immune Deficiency Syndrome) came on the scene in the 1970's that the immune system's complexity and interactions began to be thoroughly examined and understood. Quite simply, the immune system is the body's army against illness. This militia is composed of organs, cells and communication equipment that organize efficient search and destroy missions.

Fast Fact

It's believed that toxic chemicals in the body can reduce immune capacity by 50%.

Did You Know...

Researchers have discovered tiny carbon particles - from the exhausts of all vehicles - lodged in the lungs of children only 3 months old!

The main soldiers, known as white blood cells, go to battle every day against a host of viruses, bacteria and other foreign invaders. These soldiers are in constant battle - guarding the organs and cells of the body, fighting off disease and maintaining optimal health. Of course, like a real army, if the soldiers are overworked and tired, they lose their ability to fight the enemy. When your immune system is overworked and weak from body pollution, poor nutrition or stress, it can't keep up with the elimination of foreign invaders.

In fact, in its confusion, the immune system can sometimes attack the very body it was meant to defend. This is exactly what happens with auto-immune diseases such as multiple sclerosis, lupus and rheumatoid arthritis. One of the first signs of a stressed immune system is the inability to fight off colds and the flu the way you once could. While popping an over-the-counter pill relieves the symptoms, it doesn't help put the immune system back in order! It actually becomes another source of body pollution. With a healthy immune system, chances are you won't get sick even after being exposed to viruses. With a compromised immune system, you're a sitting duck for whatever you come in contact with.

Body pollution sources such as ultra violet sunlight, pesticides and smog, chemicals such as dioxins and PCB's, as well as contaminated drinking water can all have a destructive effect on the immune system. Quite possibly, the greatest damage to the body occurs when the immune system is overworked and less efficient due to the onslaught of body pollution and poor nutrition. We're seeing the evidence of this today in the alarming increase of immune related conditions such as allergies, asthma, chronic fatigue (ME) and arthritis.

If you want to know how the environment is affecting your health, take a look at the increasing rates of modern diseases such as cancer and heart disease. Maybe you can relate to this hypothetical case history:

Laura is a primary school teacher who seems to come down with every bug going - and working with children, there are a lot of bugs! She has several colds each winter and last winter, she was off work for a few weeks with pneumonia. After taking antibiotics, she noticed that she was even more susceptible to anything she came in contact with. Laura's daughter has recurring ear infections. Laura has observed that the children she teaches seem less healthy now than they were when she was growing up. There's certainly been a huge increase in asthma cases. One of the children in her class has cancer and several have attention deficit and other learning problems. Laura's colleagues tell her that these increases are simply because we now know how to diagnose such things but she thinks it's more than this.

Do you get the sense that our children are paying the price of pollution? There's no question that children today are not as healthy as the preceding generation - body pollution is affecting them too.

Cancer

In both adults and children, cancer rates are definitely increasing - the World Health Organization estimates there are about 10 million cases each year. 10 million new cases of this disease, which a few hundred years ago was unheard of! Is it simply because we live longer now so eventually we get cancer - or is it a consequence of our build up of body pollution?

Fast Fact

People born in the 1940's had double the rate of cancer as those born during the years 1888-1897.

The rise in cancer can be attributed to the fact that almost everything we come in contact with daily - free radicals, hormones, pesticides - is carcinogenic. Your body does its best to repair the damage caused by these foreign elements that it was never designed to handle. But in the process of cellular repair, the risk for error or mutations (i.e. cancerous cells) increases. A buildup of these mutations can cause cancer or birth defects.

Of particular interest is the fact that levels of certain toxins have been confirmed to be higher in the fat tissues of women with breast cancer. Not only were these toxins higher in the fat tissue, but the cancerous tissues themselves actually contained higher levels of chemicals such as PCB's and DDE. Remember - we've all got some of these chemicals stored in our fatty tissue. In other words, we're all at risk.

Fast Fact

One in three North American women will be diagnosed with cancer during their lifetime.

Heart Disease

Did You Know...

Breathing air contaminated with pollutants from car and truck exhaust at levels commonly found in urban areas can narrow blood vessels, even in healthy people, and potentially explain why the rate of heart attacks increases with exposure to air pollution.

While cancer is a word that strikes fear in our hearts, we need to keep in mind that it's still heart disease that is the number one killer. The average 50 year old woman is three times more likely to suffer from heart disease than breast cancer during her lifetime. Heart disease alone contributes to one third of all global deaths. Not surprising when you consider that one in every two men will develop heart disease.

Sadly, researchers are finding that coronary heart disease can begin to show up in children as young as 5-8 years old. Imagine - by the time a child is 5 years old, he or she could be showing early signs of heart disease. This rarely has anything to do with genetics and everything to do with our modern environment and diet.

Although we know that diet is a major factor in heart disease, we still eat obscene amounts of artery clogging foods. And once you've consumed those fries, the oxidized oils cause free radical damage to cells all over your body - including your blood vessels, a major factor in heart disease. That thought makes them a little less tempting!

A recent Toronto study concluded that a major artery in the arm is constricted significantly when people are exposed to smog for only two hours. Wouldn't it then just make sense that smaller arteries around the heart are also constricted when exposed to air pollution? So the heart ends up being under assault not only from what we eat but from the outside environment as well.

Taking a quick look at the body pollution diagram found at the end of this chapter will show you clearly just how you can be affected by body pollution. It impacts every aspect of health and leads to premature aging by placing a strain on virtually every system in the body. Body pollution is, unfortunately, very real and there's no avoiding it, but you can take control of how it affects your health.

Fast Fact

In Canada, 5000 premature deaths per year are linked to air pollution while increasing air pollution in Hong Kong results in 2000 premature deaths per year from respiratory diseases.

The first step is learning to be responsible for your own health. While modern medicine is excellent when it comes to dramatic life-saving interventions and engineering feats such as replacement hips and knees, it drops the ball when it comes to prevention. Physicians are kept so busy trying to keep illness under control they rarely have the time (and sometimes not the training) to consider prevention. We're much more focused on treating the symptoms or the illness after the fact rather than the root cause.

To be fair, doctors are facing an uphill battle when it comes to educating their patients on health and disease prevention. Commercials that promote junk food are everywhere and these foods are often sold in schools and even children's hospitals. Air and water pollution affect every place on earth. Our culture is rooted in convenience rather than based on health-promoting principles.

On the plus side, modern medicine does provide us with many interventions that can both prolong life and maintain quality of life. We've also come a long way in our understanding of the body and nutrition and this understanding is still growing.

Think of all our current conveniences, would you really want to go back in time - even if the air was cleaner then? Most of us appreciate the wonders of modern life such as airplanes, microwaves, computers, central heating and so on.

For those who'd rather give up modern conveniences to live in a pure world - it's really not an option. Not all of us can live in Biosphere 2. We need to take measures to protect our health and heal the damages of body pollution. Luckily, there are ways to do that.

Okinawans, a population in Japan, have among the lowest mortality rates in the world. As a result, they enjoy not only what may be the world's longest life expectancy but the world's longest health expectancy. Those who reach over 100 years of age in particular, have a history of aging slowly and delaying or escaping entirely the chronic diseases of aging including dementia, cardiovascular disease (coronary heart disease and stroke) and cancer.

Okinawans are very much in control of their health and live a long, healthy and active life. If they can do it, you can do it too - take charge of your health - it is, after all, your birthright. Don't accept that you have to age at the same rate as others around you. Don't assume that getting older means being

Health Tip

Fish is an excellent food, filled with nutrients, but unfortunately, they suffer from body pollution too and can be a source of heavy metals - limit consumption to no more than twice a week.

inactive or having debilitating diseases. Don't put up with less than optimal health.

Conclusion

Your body is the greatest healer of all. Give it the tools it needs to stay in excellent health by deciding today that you are going to make a commitment to reclaim your health and to fight body pollution. Let's get started…

Take Action Today

1. *Become aware of what you put in your body - ask yourself "is this contributing to body pollution"?*

2. *Realize that being healthy and active well into old age is a reality and that illness and disease don't have to be a part of living.*

3. *Read on to learn about lifestyle changes that can help you take control of you health and fight body pollution.*

Diagram 2-1: Body Pollution   Chapter 2

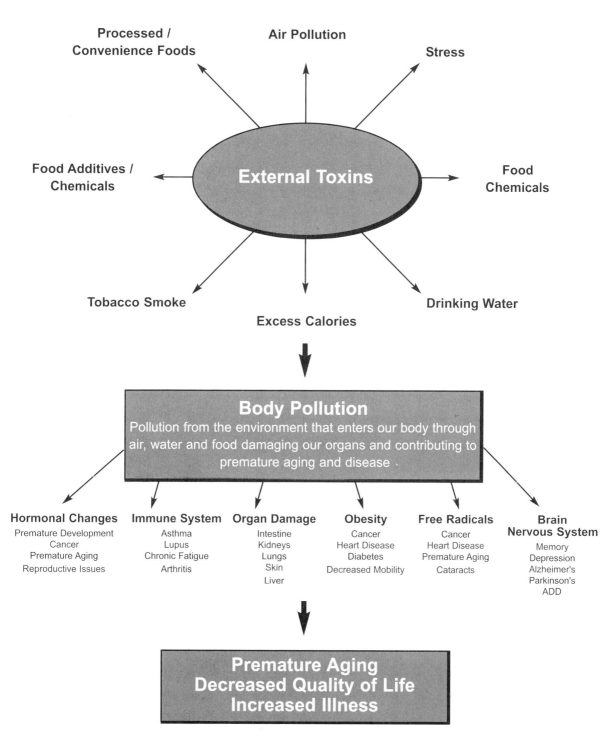

CHAPTER 3

Fighting Back With Good Nutrition

So far, I've given you a clear picture of the body pollution that every living being is confronted with today and the long term impact as well as the ripple effect it can have on you and your health. The entire point of this book is to prove to you that you can put yourself back in charge of your health and your future.

One of the most important actions to take to live a healthy life is to be informed about nutrition. These days, that's not easy. The whole subject is complex enough to make your head spin. 'Eat this, don't eat that. No, that's okay, but avoid this. Whoops! We were wrong. Start all over.' It's no wonder people get confused and simply throw up their hands in defeat. You'll get contradictory advice from anyone you talk to, including many nutritionists.

That's because the study of nutrition is still fairly new and more information comes out every day. While all of this information is quite complicated, it leads us back to the simple concept that to maintain health and prevent disease, we must return to a more nutritious diet. As you read this book, and become well-informed, you'll find that staying healthy can actually be fairly simple and straightforward. So hang in there! The returns are well worth the effort.

If survival is all you're looking for then enough food and water will do the trick. If thriving at optimal level is what you're striving for, you'll need to do more than just the basics. Bodies, similar to cars, are made up of many intricate parts. Just as cars need fuel, oil, coolant, engine fluid, etc., our bodies also need many different ingredients to function optimally. Your body is an amazing machine, yet unfortunately, many of us take better care of our cars. This is strange, since a car is expected to only last a few years, but your body lasts an entire lifetime. How would you treat your car if you could only have one for your entire life? Doesn't your body deserve the best of care along with premium fuel?

Did You Know...

During the refining process of whole wheat, the grain is bleached, sometimes using a bleaching agent similar to laundry bleach.

Fast Fact

You have to eat 8 oranges today to get the same level of vitamin A that your grandmother got from just one orange.

If you take a look at the diets of our ancestors, you'll see that they were made up of exactly the nutrients the body needs - water, carbohydrate, healthy fat and protein. You'll also find it contained vitamins, minerals and other plant nutrients. This is no coincidence and no surprise. The compounds of healthy whole foods are the building blocks your body needs to function. Let's take a closer look:

Table 3-1: The Body's Building Blocks

Building Block	Role in Body
Protein (amino acids)	Building material for the growth and maintenance of muscle, bone and other body tissues, enzymes, hormones, transportation, immune system
Carbohydrate └► Fibre	Energy Cleansing, satiety
Healthy Fats	Energy, hormones, cell membranes
Vitamins	Assist enzymes that release energy from carbohydrate, fat and protein. Prevent deficiency, support optimal health. Antioxidants
Minerals	Assist enzymes in diverse tasks all over the body. Antioxidants
Plant Nutrients	Antioxidants, Detoxifiers, Immune support

It's just common sense that eating well and providing your body with the proper fuel will keep you healthy. Are you giving your body all the building blocks it needs? Does the average person eat well enough to stay healthy? Does our modern diet supply us with the nutrients we need to thrive?

The answer is more than likely no - especially considering the additional assault we're constantly under from our polluted environment.

Fast Fact

While 75% of Canadians believe they eat well, the fact is only one in six eats the recommended number of fruits and vegetables every day and only one in twenty has a daily diet that includes the recommended amount of whole grains.

Our Changing Diet

Over the past few centuries there have been dramatic changes in our modern diet thanks in part to food processing techniques, soil depletion, food chemicals and the growing popularity of high calorie fast foods with little nutritional value. While we will never rid our diet of these changes, it is important to be aware of what we are consuming and what healthy alternatives are available to us.

Refined Flour

Bread was once known as 'the staff of life'. I'm quite sure they were not talking about that enriched, white bread that you see on the supermarket shelves today. In fact, before the nineteenth century we were still eating whole wheat bread and white flour was reserved for royalty or the wealthy. In 1876, in Paris, the first light white French rolls were made available at an exposition that the governor of Minnesota attended. He wanted others to have access to this great new discovery.

On his return to America, he developed the steel roller mills, which separated the bran and germ from the wheat, producing huge volumes of fine white flour. The advantage was it could be stored (not even the rats or worms were interested in it!) without becoming rancid. As the huge roller mills became widely adopted, the small local stone mills went out of business and white flour and white bread became food for the masses.

As the use of white flour became widespread, nutrient deficiency diseases such as beriberi, pellagra and anemia became so prevalent, health officials urged the milling industry to return the bran and germ to the flour.

Health Tip

Olive and canola oil are the best choices for cooking oils because they contain the highest levels of polyunsaturated fats - the healthiest fats.

Did You Know...

Certain essential fats are involved in the signaling of hormones and also play a role in regulating the immune system.

But the genie was already out of the bottle. The millers had developed a lucrative market for these discarded by-products of the milling process and sold the bran and germ for animal feed. Still, health problems were so persistent that the millers were persuaded to "enrich" the long lasting white flour. Don't be mislead into thinking that "enriched" means that the nutritional value of the original food has been restored. Here's the real truth:

Refined white flour is missing up to 80% of the nutrients found in the original wheat kernel. Vitamins and minerals are reduced by approximately 75% and the fibre content is only 7% of what it used to be. The tiny bit of vitamin E left after refining is destroyed through the bleaching process. The 'enriching' process, although not the same in every country, only adds back a few of these missing nutrients, sometimes as little as 4 of the 13 essential vitamins and one mineral. Makes you wonder how they can call this 'enriched'. So, next time, reach for whole wheat when you're buying flour or bread.

Table 3-2: Nutrients lost when wheat flour is refined

Nutrient	% Lost	Nutrient	% Lost	Nutrient	% Lost
Cobalt	88.5	Zinc	77.7	Copper	67.9
Vitamin E	86.3	Thiamin	77.1	Calcium	60.0
Manganese	85.8	Potassium	77.0	Pantothenic Acid	50.0
Magnesium	84.7	Iron	75.6	Molybdenum	48.0
Niacin	80.8	Vitamin B6	71.8	Chromium	40.0
Riboflavin	80.0	Phosphorus	70.9	Selenium	15.9
Sodium	78.3	Fibre	93		

Processed Oil

With modern processing techniques, oil can be pressed in high quantities much more easily than ever before. This increase in accessibility has caused a dramatic rise in the amount of fat our diets contain. These days almost anything can be fried.

Some unsaturated fats or healthy fats are necessary for good health. The trouble is, although we're consuming a high fat diet we're still deficient in essential good fats.

Many modern processing techniques are used to prevent fats from being oxidized or becoming rancid. The problem is, many of these techniques destroy the healthy essential fats and often leave behind unhealthy compounds.

One of the unhealthiest modern oil processes is called hydrogenation which involves a reaction that adds hydrogen to fats. The advantage of fully or partially hydrogenating an oil is that it protects against oxidation (prolongs shelf life) and alters the texture of foods so as an example, vegetable oils can become spreadable margarine.

While this process is advantageous to manufacturers, it is detrimental to our health as it turns healthy unsaturated fats into saturates. Another disadvantage of partial hydrogenation is that some of the fat molecules become what are known as 'trans fats'. Both saturated, and trans fats have been implicated in increased risk of heart disease.

The average person consumes 12 g per day of hydrogenated fats even though guidelines suggest that no more than 2% (approximately 4 grams) of our fat intake should come from this source.

Did You Know...

Salt and smoke have been used as preservatives since early history. The Egyptians used colours and flavourings to preserve their food while the Romans used saltpeter, and spices.

Fast Fact

Four or five grams of trans fat a day over a period of 14 years will increase your heart-disease risk by 100 percent.

Not only is this consumption of processed fats a risk factor for disease, in addition to this, don't forget that consuming too much of any fat increases your storage area for toxins. The fat we carry around then becomes our own customized toxic waste dump!

Sugar

Refined flour and processed fats are not the only culprits in today's diet. Excess sugar is another. Sugar in its raw form, or how it used to be consumed by our ancestors, was nothing like how it is today. Again, processing has depleted it of any nutritional value leaving us with the sugar we regularly consume so much of today. Sugar is added to almost any packaged food you buy today, not to mention the vast amounts of sugary sweets and beverages available to satisfy our 'sweet tooth'. The average person now consumes roughly 20 teaspoons of added sugar per day - twice the amount recommended by health experts. Let's see, that adds up to 34 pounds or 15 kilos per year and if you multiply that by 80 years, then the average person consumes a staggering amount of 2,720 pounds (1236 kgs) - over one ton - of sugar in a lifetime. In our frenzy to cut back on fats, we've substituted sugar.

Health Tip

Eating a small amount of protein at each meal will help stabilize blood sugar levels and prevent sugar cravings.

Carbonated soft drinks are the single biggest source of refined sugar in the modern diet.

These high sugar foods contribute to our calorie intake but have virtually no nutritional value. So we gain weight but are malnourished. Foods that are low in nutritional value are often called empty calories. When we eat too many empty calories, we neglect eating the nutritious fruits, vegetables and whole grains that help us to fight body pollution.

Food Chemicals

We've seen what's been taken out of our food now let's look at what's being added through modern food processing techniques. Food chemicals/additives are used to enhance flavor, colour, and shelf life. That's fine so far - but the trouble is they add a lot more than we bargained for!

More than 10,000 food chemicals are approved for use in our food today.

In the past, food additives were so costly only the rich could afford them but recently, new substances have been discovered which are relatively inexpensive. Along with that, new developments in technology make additives easier to produce. So now they're everywhere in every imaginable form! Ever wonder how food can travel halfway around the globe and still look and taste good? Chemicals are the answer and they're very definitely a mixed blessing.

One example is the preservative nitrite which is found in smoked or cured meat. While it extends the life of these meats, it is of particular concern since it's been linked to the formation of carcinogens in the body. The good news is that taking enough vitamin C will help to inhibit the formation of these cancer causing chemicals that nitrites produce. Next time you're invited to a barbecue, take along your vitamin C!

Like many of our modern conveniences, we can't completely avoid food additives. What is important is to be aware of them, give your body the nutrients it needs to minimize the effects of this form of body pollution.

Fast Foods

Fast food consumption is on the rise around the world. In the 1960's, there were only a few fast food restaurants - today there are tens of thousands in existence with thousands more opening up each year. Obviously there is demand to support this booming industry. We are all guilty of the occasional fast food meal, but when it becomes a regular part of the diet, it is hardly the fuel your body needs to stay healthy.

What people don't realize is that fast food meals include all aspects of modern food processing. These meals are typically high in calories and contain little nutritional value. Most fast foods are made of refined ingredients making them devoid of vitamins, minerals and fibre. Fried foods are high in artery clogging fats, and your super sized soft drink is loaded with little except sugar. It's definitely fast, and cheap but not exactly your ideal body pollution-fighting diet.

Fighting Body Pollution Lifestyle Pyramid

Maybe you do your best to follow a balanced diet. While this is a good start, there is much more you can do to provide your body with the fuel it needs to function at peak performance.

There are many theories put forth by nutrition experts about what we should and shouldn't eat. What is perhaps most simple, is to look at what our ancestors ate or in other words, what the human body was programmed to eat - a natural, balanced diet consisting of lean meats, healthy fats, fruits and vegetables and clean water. In addition to a good diet, a healthy lifestyle including exercise can also encourage a disease free, active life.

With this in mind, I've designed the ultimate fighting body pollution lifestyle pyra-

Did You Know...

In 1970, Americans spent approximately 6 billion dollars on fast food and in 2000 they spent more than 110 billion dollars.

Health Tip

An easy way to avoid unhealthy fats: the more solid fats are at room temperature, the more they should be avoided.

mid. Using this as a guideline, you will find that eating right and living a healthy lifestyle is actually quite simple. Choose foods and activities that fall near the bottom of the pyramid most often, and limit those that are close to the top. You'll notice that fruits, vegetables, pure water, exercise and supplements form the foundation of the pyramid - this is because these are essential components in the fight against body pollution.

Diagram 3-1: Fighting Body Pollution Lifestyle Pyramid

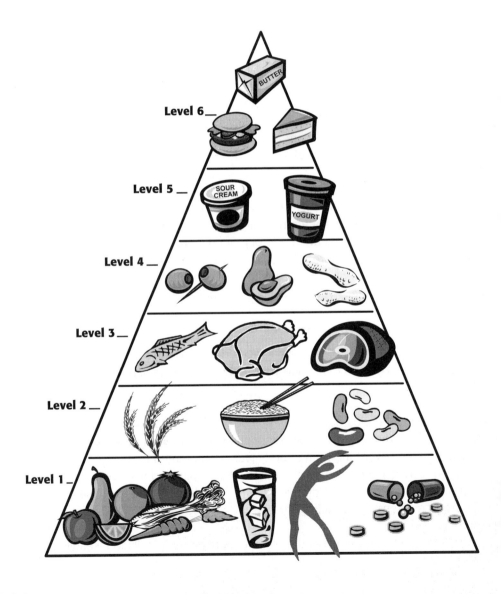

Level 1 - Fruits and Vegetables:

- Research has shown that a diet rich in plant foods helps to prevent chronic disease.
- Fruits and vegetables are a rich source of vitamins, minerals, antioxidants and plant nutrients - all vital in fighting body pollution.
- A diet supporting optimal health should contain at least 5 - 10 servings of fruits and vegetables per day.
- Choose a variety of dark green and brightly coloured fruits and vegetables.

Water:

- The human body is 90% water.
- Replenishing the body with water assists with regulation, digestion and cleansing.
- Drink at least 8 glasses of pure filtered or bottled water per day.

Exercise:

- Exercise is an equally fundamental part of optimal health. It is essential in weight maintenance, disease prevention and assists the body in its cleansing process.
- Incorporate exercise into your daily routine. This should include both aerobic exercise and weight or resistance training.

Nutritional Supplements:

- It is impossible to get all the nutrients we need from diet alone. These days, even a well-balanced diet, although still very important, is just not enough.
- In order to fight body pollution, it is essential to arm your body with whole foods and supplements including, vitamins, minerals, botanicals, antioxidants and plant nutrients.

Did You Know...

It takes about 16,000 steps to walk off a typical fast-food meal (790 calories) or just over two hours of brisk walking. For a super size meal, count on a three-hour walk, preferably uphill.

Level 2 - Whole Grains:

- Whole grains are an excellent source of fibre, vitamins and minerals - excellent tools in fighting body pollution.
- Fibre works to assist the body in cleansing, and promotes satiety.
- Choose whole grain products rather than "white" or enriched.

Legumes:

- According to research, increasing legume intake (chickpeas, lentils, kidney beans, fava beans, peanuts, navy beans, lima beans, string beans, and split peas) may be an important dietary intervention to reduce chronic disease.
- Legumes are an excellent source of both fibre and protein.

Level 3 - Lean Meats, Poultry and Fish:

- Protein is an important part of a healthy diet for tissue growth, repair and maintenance.
- Lean meats and poultry can be an excellent source of protein. Always remove skin from chicken.
- Fish is a good source of protein and healthy fats. Salmon, herring, and mackerel are excellent sources of healthy fats (omega 3 fatty acids).

Level 4 - Plant Oils and Healthy Fats:

- Not all oils or fats are bad. In fact, some fats are quite essential to good health, especially the heart. These are found in many plants as well as some fish.
- When choosing cooking oils, stick to mono and poly-unsaturated fats. The leading choices are olive and flax oils, followed by canola oil for cooking.

Nuts:

- Nuts are an important source of fibre, and they are loaded with essential minerals and vitamins - especially the antioxidants vitamin E and selenium.
- Nuts also contain protein necessary for normal growth and development.
- Consuming nuts in moderation can be an excellent high energy addition to a healthy diet.

Level 5 - Low-Fat Dairy and Fermented Food Products:

- Low-fat dairy products can be an excellent source of many vitamins and minerals especially calcium.
- Fermented foods and beverages such as yogurt, kefir and soft cheese can be excellent food sources for healthy digestion by restoring healthy intestinal bacteria.
- These healthy bacteria are an important line of defense against invading viruses, yeasts, parasites and pathogenic bacteria.

Level 6 - Processed Fats:

- Although all fats should be eaten in moderation, trans and saturated fats should be avoided whenever possible.
- Processed fats (heated, hydrogenated etc.) should be strictly limited in a healthy diet.
- Limit butter, margarine, mayonnaise etc. and other high-fat products.
- Limit frying of foods - try steaming or sautéing instead.

Sweets and Convenience Foods:

- Sweets and convenience foods can form part of a healthy diet if consumed in limited amounts.
- Limit fast foods and highly processed food - choose whole foods instead.
- Limit intake of sweets, soft drinks and refined sugars.

Conclusion

I hope I've convinced you of the need to take charge of your health and also shown you that it can be a fairly simple process. It's really just a matter of being informed and making some changes in your lifestyle - starting with good nutrition. You can begin to incorporate dietary changes into your daily routine immediately and you should start to see and feel the effects in a few weeks. The difference in your energy level and your appearance can be dramatic.

Even the best diet can't provide the level and variety of nutrients that we need to protect us from the environment we live in. In fact, a typical diet just provides us with the absolute bare minimum required for survival. Making food choices as outlined in our lifestyle pyramid is a vital step in the right direction, but it's still not enough. Nutritional supplements can help you bridge the gap between the nutrients your body needs and what even the best diet cannot provide.

Supplements, a healthy lifestyle, including exercise, and smart food choices are your ultimate weapons in the fight against body pollution.

Take Action Today

1. *Revamp your daily routine according to the Fighting Body Pollution Lifestyle Pyramid.*

2. *Go through your cupboards and throw out your junk food. Read the ingredients first - can you believe you actually ate that stuff?*

3. *Drink plenty of purified water - hydration is important to the body's cleansing process.*

CHAPTER

Vitamins: What's in a Name?

Did You Know...

Unlike most animals, human beings can neither manufacture nor store vitamin C. Our requirements must be met from dietary sources such as citrus fruit, vegetables, and supplements.

Plenty, as it turns out. For the history buffs among you, the origin of vitamins is a fascinating story. By the 18th century, scientists were starting to realize the relationship between vitamins and health. They had discovered that adding citrus fruits to a diet would prevent scurvy.

British sailors turned out to be the unwitting guinea pigs. After three months on a long ocean trip, eating nothing but meat and cereals, the sailors began coming down with strange symptoms such as bleeding and swollen gums, swollen legs and arms, bleeding in the eyes, very dry skin, shortness of breath and hair loss. Some men were incapacitated and many died.

Once British ships were supplied with lime juice and marmalade, their illness - scurvy - disappeared and they became known as 'limeys'. What they didn't realize is that they were replenishing their bodies with vitamin C. Interestingly, another term for vitamin C is 'ascorbic acid', which happens to be Latin for 'without scurvy'.

This was a dramatic breakthrough but generally speaking, scientific understanding of nutritional principles progressed slowly. By the time the 20th century rolled around, scientists realized that substituting unpolished rice for processed rice would prevent beriberi, a vitamin B deficiency disease. The polished rice lacked vitamin B1 (Thiamin), which proved to be crucial in maintaining health. The Polish chemist Casimir Funk discovered that the anti-beriberi substance in unpolished rice was an amine (a type of nitrogen-containing compound) so he called it vitamine - for vital amine. It was later discovered that many vitamins don't contain amines at all but the name stuck - without the 'e'.

In 1906 the British scientist Frederick Hopkins proved that foods contained vital elements besides proteins, carbohydrates, fats, minerals and water. Scientists, including Hopkins and Funk, isolated and identified vitamins after experimenting with animals by depriving them of certain foods and measuring the results. In 1912, Hopkins and Funk figured out that the absence of specific vitamins could lead to certain diseases. This might not seem so earth-shattering now but a hundred years ago, it was groundbreaking research.

It would be nice to report that our understanding of nutrition over the centuries has always taken us forward, but that's not true. While generally there has been significant groundbreaking research done, some fallacies have also gained popularity.

Consider that just thirty years ago, in North American hospitals, patients in the intensive care cardiac unit were fed bacon and eggs for breakfast! A high-protein, high-fat diet was considered by many, including health professionals, to be very healthy. Today, many of us know better.

Our knowledge of nutrition and food has increased enormously in the past thirty years, but there are still many misconceptions firmly fixed in the average person's mind. One fallacy that stubbornly persists is the idea that vitamins are a source of energy. They're not - but they do help regulate the body's metabolism so it can use and release energy from food.

Some vitamins also work with enzymes, helping the body with growth, maintenance and repair. There are 13 different vitamins, all of which are essential to good health because they cannot be made by the body. A basic knowledge of them is critical when it comes to staying healthy.

Fast Fact

In the Health Professional follow up study, men who took multivitamins with folate (folic acid) for more than 10 years had a 25% reduction in colon cancer risk.

Vitamins fall into two categories - water soluble and fat soluble. Water soluble vitamins aren't stored by the body for very long and so they need to be eaten regularly. Vitamin C and the B vitamins are water soluble - excess amounts aren't stored but excreted through urine instead.

Vitamin A, D, E and K are the fat-soluble vitamins. Your diet needs to include some good fats in order to transport and store these vitamins. Excess amounts of vitamin A and D can be toxic if consumed in extremely high doses because they are stored and can build up to unhealthy levels. Most people, though, get too little, not too much. Refer to the vitamin chart at the end of this chapter to learn about specific vitamin roles and doses.

Are You Getting Enough Vitamins from Your Diet?

Although people in developed countries tend to think they're getting all the vitamins they need from their diet alone, that's not necessarily so. In fact, you'll find that the richer countries of the world often harbour very serious hidden cases of malnutrition because they have access to an abundance of food that appeases the appetite without really supplying nutrients. Canadian research shows that only one in six Canadians gets enough fruits and vegetables and worse, only one in twenty gets the recommended amount of grain products - these are the foods rich in nutrients our bodies need regularly.

Most countries have guidelines to help you know how much of certain vitamins you need. Many of these guidelines were based around the US Recommended Dietary Allowances (RDA).

Let me tell you how these came about. The RDA's were originally set up by the National Academy of Sciences, during World War II, as general guidelines for feeding the country's soldiers. They were then further used to ensure that healthy people under optimal circumstances (i.e., no illness, no genetic weaknesses, no environmental toxin exposure) would not develop nutritional deficiencies resulting in diseases such as scurvy or beriberi. Today, of course, preventing deficiency is not enough. Research is showing everyday that vitamins are implicated in much more than just deficiency, and in fact, higher levels are needed for optimal health and the prevention of modern day chronic diseases such as cancer, cardiovascular disease and cataracts - just to name a few. The RDA only guarantees a minimal rather than an optimal level of nutrition.

The sad truth is that many people all over the world don't even meet the minimal levels outlined in the RDA guidelines. Each person is unique with different

Did You Know...

Vitamin D is unique because it can be manufactured by the body only in the presence of sunlight. If you live in a smoggy city, you may not be getting the vitamin D you need since the smog absorbs the sun's ultraviolet rays.

nutritional requirements at different times in their lives, so even the most conscientious and well-informed person might not be getting everything that his or her body needs.

Take a look at some of the conditions that require an additional nutritional boost:

• Adolescence	• Emotional or Physical Stress	• Pregnancy
• Aging	• Exhaustion	• Nursing Mother
• Illness	• Alcohol Consumption	• Rapid Physical Growth
• Athletic activity	• Menstruation	• Time Change
• Dieting	• Menopause	• Travel
• Smoking	• Overwork	

Health Tip

Men and Women over the age of 50 should avoid excessive levels of iron in their supplement. Look for a multi-vitamin & mineral supplement with less than 5 mg of iron.

This is by no means a complete list and I haven't even touched on body pollution - those internal and external toxins which, in fact, are the biggest threat of all to your health.

You can see that while dramatic vitamin deficiencies such as scurvy and beriberi are now uncommon in developed countries, a less than optimal intake of certain vitamins is almost standard, particularly among the elderly. According to a recent USDA survey more than 80 percent of women and 70 percent of men consumed less than two-thirds of the very conservative RDA recommendations for one or more nutrients. No wonder chronic diseases are on the rise!

Here are just some of the problems that can arise when we don't get the nutrition we need. Low levels of vitamin D can lead to osteoporosis and bone fractures. Research showed that 50% of a group of postmenopausal women admitted to hospital with hip fractures were deficient in vitamin D. Sixty-two percent of female adolescents in Finland in the winter had low vitamin D concentrations and 13% were deficient. Low levels of the antioxidant vitamins (beta carotene, E and C) may increase risk for several chronic diseases such as cancer, arthritis and heart disease.

Fast Fact

Supplementing with folic acid, vitamins B12 and B6 can reduce the risk of heart disease by 50% by maintaining healthy levels of homocysteine in the blood.

A lack of folic acid and vitamins B6 and B12 is now known to place you at risk for cardiovascular disease, colon and breast cancer. Folic acid is even more crucial for pregnant women - a deficiency has been associated with a greater risk of the baby being born with spina bifida. In fact, if all women of child-bearing age used multi-vitamins with folic acid, neural tube birth defects such as spina bifida would be reduced by about 70%.

Vitamin Supplements

The fact is that most people don't get an optimal amount of all the vitamins they require by their diet alone and need to take supplements as a safeguard.

In saying that, I've now got a powerful ally on my side. While the highly influential and much respected *Journal of the American Medical Association* insisted for years that we can get all the nutrients we need from our diet, they have finally changed their mind.

While this change-of-heart may not seem revolutionary to the average lay person who's known for years that diet alone is not sufficient to meet all one's nutritional needs, it is a huge breakthrough on the part of the medical establishment.

This respected journal is the voice of the entire American Medical Association and their recommendation to use a supplement daily is a powerful shift in conventional thinking. They have completely reversed their previous stand and now recommend that all adults take at least one multi-vitamin daily. This is one giant step forward!

Not only that, the ultra-conservative American Medical Association has endorsed the idea that what we eat is a central component of an overall program of preventive health care. I'm hoping that this means that doctors will begin to look more closely at the eating habits of their patients. These organizations don't move quickly, but the progress that's being made is very encouraging.

This new awareness is part of a slow but growing attitude shift in conventional medicine when it comes to nutritional supplements. The prevailing opinion used to be that vitamin supplements weren't needed since the typical diet provides all that we need to maintain good health. But it's clear, even to an informed layperson, that we don't always eat what we need.

Did You Know...

Most women who take oral contraceptives are unaware that the pill can interfere with the processing of vitamins B6, B12, folic acid and vitamin C.

Natural Versus Synthetic Vitamins

The difference between "synthetic' and "natural" vitamins can be confusing. While it's always better to get vitamins from whole foods, we've seen that this just isn't happening. When people rely on diet alone for their nutritional requirements, vitamin deficiencies are commonplace.

Health Tip

When buying a vitamin E supplement, check the label carefully and look for the natural source d- form - avoid the synthetic dl- form.

When considering a vitamin supplement, ensure that wherever possible, the supplement contains a natural source of the vitamin. The natural source of vitamin E is particularly important since it's absorbed 40% more efficiently than the synthetic form.

Most high-quality vitamin-mineral supplements also have non-medicinal ingredients similar to those found in whole foods that help with absorption. Bioflavonoids, for example, are compounds found in many vitamin C rich foods that are thought to enhance the absorption of vitamin C as well as prolong its effectiveness.

In fact, some premium brands of vitamins include digestive enzymes that assist in absorption along with botanical extracts that provide added health benefits.

Tips for Choosing a Good Multi-vitamin

Things get confusing pretty quickly when you go to purchase a multi-vitamin. So here are some tips to guide you:

1. Choose a vitamin as close as possible to the original food source - look for natural sources.
2. Find a multi-vitamin as close as possible to the RDA for each nutrient.
3. Look for a supplement that's age and gender specific - men and women have different nutritional needs.
4. Make sure vitamins and minerals are combined in your supplement.
5. Look for a supplement that contains additional non-medicinal ingredients that help absorption of vitamins such as bioflavonoids.

Antioxidants

While all vitamins are important for health, certain vitamins act as antioxidants and are essential for protecting the body from the damages of body pollution. Antioxidants are compounds found in foods and supplements that neutralize free radicals. You'll recall from Chapter Two that free radicals, when produced in excess cause damage to your cells and contribute to premature aging and disease. In order to defend against these damaging molecules, your body has a very complicated antioxidant defense system that uses antioxidants from the diet to clear out free radicals and prevent damage.

Antioxidants do this in three ways: they reduce the energy of the free radical, stop it from forming in the first place or interrupt the chain reaction which minimizes the damage. While the jury is still out on whether antioxidants can prevent or treat specific diseases, their importance in maintaining good health is indisputable. Researchers believe that even the healthiest diet may not provide sufficient amounts of antioxidants, especially considering the assault we're under on a daily basis from body pollution. Each time antioxidants are used to neutralize free radicals, the body's supply diminishes - it is very important to keep it replenished.

So good nutrition and optimal health also means getting enough antioxidants from your diet. While most antioxidants are concentrated in brightly coloured berries, fruits and vegetables, you'll find that many different compounds can act as antioxidants including vitamins, herbs and minerals, to mention a few.

Vitamins C, E and beta carotene (provitamin A) act as antioxidants and provide essential protection from free radicals.

Since these vitamins are so important, let's look at them up close to see exactly how they help maintain our health.

Vitamin C

Scurvy, a severe deficiency of vitamin C that can result in death, has been beaten. Or has it? Some of these diseases that we believed were long gone are coming back to haunt us. It's shocking to realize that much of the severe degeneration in seniors can be attributed to near-scurvy levels of vitamin C. Vitamin C is water soluble so you need to replenish your supply every day because your body doesn't retain it.

It seems that not a day goes by without more exciting research showing more benefits of vitamin C. For one thing, researchers have found that people who suffer from asthma, arthritis, cancer, diabetes and heart disease have lower levels of vitamin C in their blood than the average person.

Health Tip

Vitamin C helps in the absorption of non-animal forms of iron such as the iron found in fruits, vegetables and nuts.

Did You Know...

During the Alaskan Klondike gold rush, (1897-1898) potatoes were worth their weight in gold. They were so valued for their vitamin C content that miners traded gold for potatoes.

Fast Fact

Just one cigarette destroys 25-100 mg of vitamin C.

Current research also shows that vitamin C reduces the risk of developing cataracts and other eye diseases. In fact, very recently, the age-related Eye Disease Studies reported that a daily mixture of the antioxidant vitamins (E, C and beta carotene with zinc) slowed the progression of macular degeneration, one of the major causes of blindness in the elderly. Until this groundbreaking research, there was very little that could be done to halt or treat the disease.

Knowing that eye conditions can be prevented nutritionally is welcome news to an aging population. So you have a choice - you can meet your nutritional requirements now or pay for it later by developing a chronic illness or condition that then needs to be treated with drugs.

Vitamin C has also been shown to lower blood pressure and cholesterol which means it helps to prevent heart attacks. Another way vitamin C appears to protect against heart disease is by reducing the stiffness of arteries and the tendency of platelets to clump together. Scientists at the European Prospective Investigation into Cancer and Nutrition found that low blood levels of vitamin C may result in a higher risk of heart attack and stroke in men and women and some cancers in men.

Vitamin C's antioxidant properties are thought to protect smokers as well as those exposed to second-hand smoke and other environmental toxins, from the harmful effects of free radicals.

Vitamin C is needed to make collagen, the "glue" that strengthens many parts of the body, such as tendons, ligaments and blood vessels. It also plays an important role in wound healing and acts as a natural antihistamine. In addition to this, it helps in the formation of liver bile as well as fighting viruses and detoxifying alcohol and other substances. You can see why we say it's essential!

This hard-working vitamin is thought to protect the body against the accumulation or retention of lead, heavy metal that can lead to brain damage, particularly in growing children.

The amount of vitamin C you need on a daily basis varies with age and nutritional status. If you smoke or are taking prescription drugs, you'll need to up your daily intake.

Vitamin E

Vitamin E, is sometimes called a 'miracle worker' and when you add up all the benefits it provides, it's easy to understand why.

Studies show that vitamin E has a beneficial effect on aging, infertility, heart disease, cancer and athletic performance. Vitamin E's antioxidant properties help to protect the body from cell damage that can lead to diverse ailments such as cancer, heart disease and cataracts.

Vitamin E works with other antioxidants such as vitamin C, to offer protection from certain chronic diseases. It also has a direct effect on inflammation, blood cell regulation, connective tissue growth and genetic control of cell division.

Vitamin E is thought to protect the body against a variety of carcinogens and toxins - including mercury, lead, carbon tetrachloride, benzene, ozone and nitrous oxide. It can also prevent the formation of nitrosamines from nitrates and nitrites found in cured meats, cigarette smoke and polluted air.

Low amounts of vitamin E have been found in people with rheumatoid arthritis. Scientists believe that the vitamin is depleted during the inflammatory process. Clinical trials have shown that high levels of vitamin E (1,200-1,800 IU per day) can decrease the inflammation and pain of arthritis.

Did You Know...

High levels of vitamin C can protect levels of vitamin E in the body and may contribute to the immune-enhancement of vitamin E.

Fast Fact

To get 100 IU (international units) of vitamin E daily, you'd need to consume over 5 cups of peanuts or 1.5 cups of corn oil daily.

Some double-blind studies have shown that vitamin E improves glucose tolerance in people with type 2 diabetes, although it may take three months or more of supplementation for the benefits to become apparent. Some researchers also believe that large amounts of vitamin E may slow the progression of Alzheimer's disease.

There's still more! Two studies show that men and women who supplement with at least 100 IU of vitamin E every day for at least two years have a 37-41% drop in the risk of heart disease. Even more impressive was the 77% drop in nonfatal heart attacks reported after participants were given 400-800 IU vitamin E each day. According to research, vitamin E seems to help prevent heart attacks, but isn't helpful in the treatment of heart conditions. So it's important to take it as a preventive measure.

Beta Carotene (also known as provitamin A)

Beta carotene is a reddish-orange pigment found in fruits, vegetables and other plants. It has two roles in the body. It can be converted into vitamin A (retinol) if the body needs more of a boost or it can act as an antioxidant and provide protection against free radicals. Beta carotene increases the number of specific infection-fighting immune cells and in fact, the more beta carotene you have in your system, the greater the increase in protective immune cells.

Recent Harvard University research showed that women who ate one additional large carrot or one-half cup of sweet potatoes (or other foods rich in beta carotene) every day slashed their risk of heart attack by 22 percent and stroke by 40 to 70 percent.

Although not a leading antioxidant in itself, beta carotene did play a major role in opening the door to antioxidant research - from it, we've gained much promising research about many strong antioxidant carotenoids and other plant nutrients.

Conclusion

Taking some vitamins without others won't work well for you in the long run. You need the full complement of all the vitamins to work together in the fight for optimal health. This is especially important in today's climate where we know we're not getting enough vitamins from our diets. Body pollution in addition to our high stress, fast-paced lifestyle can increase the body's need for vitamins. A healthy diet and a good quality vitamin supplement will ensure that you are receiving an optimal level of these essential nutrients.

Take Action Today

1. *Realize that your diet alone cannot provide your body with optimal levels of all vitamins.*

2. *Begin taking a multi-vitamin and mineral supplement daily - base your buying decision on our tips.*

3. *Remember vitamins and minerals work together - read Chapter 5 to learn about minerals.*

Table 4-1: Vitamin Chart

Vitamin	Role in the Body	Sources	Health Conditions Supported or Focus of Current Research	RDA Women	RDA Men	Antioxidant Properties
Vitamin A	Maintenance of healthy skin, eyes, bones, hair and teeth.	Liver, milk and dairy products fortified with vitamin A.	Cystic Fibrosis, Infection, Night Blindness, Bronchitis, Immune function, Ulcer, Wound healing	800(mcg RE) 2640 IU	1000(mcg RE) 3300 IU	✓
Vitamin D	Assists in the absorption and metabolism of calcium and phosphorus for strong bones and teeth.	Sunlight, vitamin D-fortified dairy products, fish oils, tuna, salmon.	Crohn's Disease, Cystic Fibrosis, Osteoporosis, Migraine headaches, Diabetes, Multiple Sclerosis	5.0 mcg 200 IU	5.0 mcg 200 IU	
Vitamin E	As an antioxidant - helps protect cell membranes, lipoproteins, fats and vitamin A from destructive oxidation. Helps protect red blood cells from damage.	Nuts, seeds, wheat germ, margarine, vegetable oils, salad dressings made with vegetable oils.	Burns, Epilepsy, Immune function, Arthritis, Diabetes, Atherosclerosis, Athletic Performance	8.0 mg	10.0 mg	✓
Vitamin K	Needed for proper blood clotting.	Green, leafy vegetables, liver.		65 mcg	80 mcg	
Vitamin C	Acts as an antioxidant. Important for maintenance of bones, teeth, collagen and blood vessels (capillaries). Enhances iron absorption, red blood cell formation.	Citrus fruits, strawberries, cantaloupe, tomatoes, broccoli, mustard greens, cauliflower, green pepper, cabbage, asparagus, potatoes.	High cholesterol, Glaucoma, Common cold/sore throat, Capillary fragility, Athletic performance, Bronchitis	60 mg	60 mg	✓

Vitamin	Role in the Body	Sources	Health Conditions Supported or Focus of Current Research	RDA Women	RDA Men	Antioxidant Properties
Vitamin B1 (Thiamin)	Releases energy from foods. Needed for normal appetite and for functioning of nervous system.	Pork, whole and enriched grains, dried beans and peas, brewer's yeast, sunflower seeds	Alzheimer's disease, Canker sores, Diabetes, Fibromyalgia, HIV support	1.1 mg	1.5 mg	
Vitamin B2 (Riboflavin)	Releases energy from foods. Necessary for healthy skin and eyes.	Liver, milk, yogurt, mushrooms, enriched grains, whole grains	Migraine headaches, Canker sores (mouth ulcers), Cataracts	1.3 mg	1.7 mg	
Vitamin B3 (Niacin)	Releases energy from foods. Aids in maintenance of skin, nervous system and proper mental functioning.	Enriched grains, whole grains, mushrooms, bran, tuna, salmon, chicken, beef, liver, peanuts.	High cholesterol, High triglycerides, Cataracts, HIV support, Multiple sclerosis	15 mg NE	19 mg NE	
Vitamin B6	Releases energy from foods. Plays a role in protein and fat metabolism. Essential for function of red blood cells and hemoglobin synthesis.	Liver, tuna, beef, pork, spinach, bananas, soybeans, sunflower seeds.	Autism, Depression, Atherosclerosis, Asthma, Age related cognitive decline	1.6 mg	2.0 mg	
Vitamin B12	Prevents pernicious anemia - necessary for healthy nervous system Involved in synthesis of genetic material (DNA).	Foods from animal organs, oysters, clams, eggs.	Depression, High homocysteine, Pernicious anemia Chronic fatigue syndrome, Infertility (male) Atherosclerosis	2.0 mcg	2.0 mcg	

Table 4-1: Vitamin Chart

Vitamin	Role in the Body	Sources	Health Conditions Supported or Focus of Current Research	RDA Women	RDA Men	Antioxidant Properties
Biotin	Releases energy from foods - plays a role in metabolism of amino acids Needed for normal hair production and growth.	Cheese, egg yolks, cauliflower, peanut butter, liver.	Brittle nails, Diabetes	30 mcg*	30 mcg*	
Pantothenic Acid	Releases energy from foods. Involved in synthesis of acetylcholine, an excitatory neurotransmitter. Needed for normal functioning of the adrenal glands.	Mushrooms, liver, broccoli, eggs. (Most foods contain some of this nutrient.)	High Cholesterol, High Triglicerides, Rheumatoid Arthritis, Athletic Performance, Sinusitis, Lupus	5 mg*	5 mg*	
Folic Acid	Necessary for proper red blood cell formation. Plays a role in the metabolism of fats, amino acids, DNA and RNA. Needed for proper cell division and protein synthesis.	Green leafy vegetables, orange juice, organ meats, sprouts, sunflower seeds.	High Homocysteine, Pregnancy, Atherosclerosis, Colon cancer	180 mcg	200 mcg	

*No RDA for these nutrients, value given is the Daily Reference Intake as per recommendation of the Food and Nutrition Board of the Institute of Medicine

+Nutrient Recommendations will vary by country.

CHAPTER

Minerals: Salt of the Earth

Health Tip

To increase absorption of vitamins and minerals, avoid coffee and other high caffeine drinks for 1 - 1.5 hours of taking a supplement.

"Do you know that most of us today are suffering from certain dangerous diet deficiencies which cannot be remedied until the depleted soils from which our foods come are brought into proper mineral balance?"

"Our soils which are seriously deficient in trace minerals, cannot produce plant life competent to maintain our needs and with the continuous cropping and shipping away of these trace minerals and concentrates, the condition becomes worse."

"Laboratory tests prove that the fruits, the vegetables, the grains, the eggs and even the milk and meats of today are not what they were a few generations ago. No man of today can eat enough fruits and vegetables to supply his system with the minerals he requires for perfect health."

"This discovery is one of the latest and most important contributions of science to the problem of human health."

United States Senate Document #264.

Sound shocking? It certainly is, and even more so when you realize that these excerpts were taken from a government document written back in 1936. Well, we can't say we haven't been warned. We just don't seem to be listening, though.

Another alarm about the state of our soil was rung in 1977 when the U.S.

Did You Know...

When vegetables are boiled, the minerals leech out of the vegetables into the water-light steaming will preserve mineral content.

Department of Agriculture claimed "in the future, we will not be able to rely anymore on our premise that the consumptions of a varied balanced diet will provide all the essential trace minerals because such a diet will be very difficult to obtain for millions of people."

Since these warnings were sounded, the situation has gotten worse and continues to deteriorate. Part of the problem of soil depletion is that we all seemed to feel that our once rich soil was infinite and so proper precautions were not taken. Modern agriculture continues to exhaust the soil by planting the same crop year after year and by using fertilizer containing only nitrogen, phosphorous and potassium. Soil erosion which occurs naturally has also robbed our rich topsoil of minerals. The result is that the food now being grown lacks some of the basic minerals needed to sustain life.

Fast Fact

Minerals make up approximately 5% of your total body weight.

It's ironic that some of the world's richest countries have some of the world's most impoverished soil. While North American soils are among the worst in the world for mineral content, the rest of the world doesn't fare much better. According to the Earth Summit held in Rio de Janeiro in 1992, Asian soil is 76% depleted, Europe is 72% depleted, South America is 76% depleted and both the U. S. and Canada are 85% depleted of minerals, compared to 100 years ago. Australia is the least depleted at 55% - still nothing to be proud of.

Why is this such a problem? Because the earth is our only source of minerals. Here's how it works: as rock formations containing minerals are broken down after years of erosion, this mineral laden dust and sand becomes part of the soil. We then get our minerals second-hand from eating plants that have grown in this soil or the meat (or eggs or milk) of plant-eating animals.

While we like to think that our soil is rich in minerals, we've been warned time and time again that it's no longer true. It has been robbed of much of its mineral wealth over the centuries and that, in turn, robs us of our health as we'll soon see.

Why You Need Minerals

In their most elementary role, certain minerals such as sodium, potassium, calcium and magnesium act as electrolytes. Electrolytes are your body's own electrical system which relies on minerals to generate and conduct billions of tiny electrical impulses. Without these impulses not a single muscle, including your heart, could function. Neither could your brain, and your cells wouldn't be able to balance your water pressure or absorb nutrients. In other words, without minerals to manage your body's basic functions, it's lights out!

In general, minerals act as triggers, activating both enzymes and vitamins for the body to use. These hard-working elements also help stabilize your cells, construct tissue, produce energy, synthesize hormones and repair some of the damage done to your cells on a daily basis.

Vitamins often get the limelight, but the truth is minerals might play an even more vital role. If you had no vitamins, your body would still be able to access some minerals. But if you had no minerals, your body couldn't access a single vitamin! While vitamins are like chameleons, changing shape and substance in the body as needed, minerals always retain their identity. Iron might combine with other molecules, but it will always be iron. Minerals are inflexible in the sense that they can never change into something else. So they never suffer from an identity crisis!

There are two types of dietary minerals - the 'macro' or major minerals and the 'micro' or trace minerals. Not surprisingly, you need more of the macro minerals such as calcium, magnesium and phosphorus, but that doesn't mean you can overlook the importance of the micro minerals. A glance at our chart at the end of this chapter will inform you about minerals and their individual role in your health.

Did You Know...

Wound healing and immune function are highly dependent on adequate levels of trace minerals.

Mineral Deficiencies

I've shown you how important minerals are, yet multiple mineral deficiencies have been found in a large percentage of the world's population. This is not too surprising when you consider our current soil quality and recall from your previous reading that our food has a number of nutrients, including minerals, processed right out of it.

Fast Fact

A recent survey shows that 95% of the North American population suffers from at least one mineral deficiency.

Here are some of the alarming deficiencies that have shown up:

Health Tip

Almonds contain more calcium than any other nut (190 mg per ½ cup/125 ml).

Did You Know...

Vitamin E strengthens the antioxidant effect of selenium - they're more powerful when taken together.

- On average, individuals only get half the amount of copper they need.
- Iodine deficiency is a global public health problem that occurs in parts of the world with iodine-deficient soils and results in goiter - a relatively harmless swelling of the neck and cretinism, a severe birth defect.
- 80% of North American women don't get nearly enough calcium and studies in Europe show that women are only getting a third of the recommended levels.
- Iron deficiency is the most common form of nutritional deficiency, especially prevalent in young children and women of childbearing age.
- In Asia and the Pacific, there are widespread deficiencies in iron, zinc and fluoride. Most serious is the lack of iron, which causes anemia in 60% of pregnant women, 50% percent of reproductive-age women and infants and 40 percent of school-age children.
- 72% of adult North Americans aren't meeting the RDA for magnesium.

If you're concerned about getting all the nutrients you need, I recommend you take a supplement that provides you with the RDA of the minerals listed in the chart. And if you have spent time looking for just the right mineral supplement, you'll be familiar with the word 'chelated'. Chelation is the process by which minerals are absorbed and simply means that they are attached to a protein molecule that carries them into the bloodstream where they can be put to good use. The word 'chelate' comes from a Greek word that means 'claw'. In the chelation process, the protein molecule actually surrounds the mineral like a claw and helps to make it available to the body.

Some mineral supplements cost more because they're in chelated form. But there's no need to pay extra. The truth is that your body automatically chelates minerals during the absorption process anyway - as long as there is also a source of protein. So take your mineral supplements with a meal that contains protein and save yourself some money.

Now let's take a close look at the role of certain minerals in your health.

Calcium

It won't surprise you to learn that calcium is the most abundant mineral in the body. Males carry about three pounds and females carry about two pounds of calcium - most of it in bones and teeth with the rest found in the soft tissues and watery parts of the body where it regulates the normal body processes. That's the kind of weight you want to fortify, not lose!

Calcium provides a great example of exactly how minerals work synergistically with vitamins, enzymes and other minerals. About 10-40% of the calcium you get from your diet is absorbed in the small intestine with the help of vitamin D. (Calcium can't be absorbed well without both vitamin D and hydrochloric acid). Magnesium is also a member of this powerful team that helps to fortify bones.

If you don't get enough calcium in your diet, the body will begin to dip into its reserves - your bones. If the deficiency goes on long enough, you'll suffer from osteoporosis. While this disease can strike at any age, older people are more vulnerable. One in four women and one in eight men over the age of 50 have osteoporosis. Eighty percent of women are deficient in calcium and this world-wide health problem costs billions of dollars to treat. This condition is much more than just a nuisance, it's a serious health problem that's easily preventable.

Did You Know...

Mineral absorption can increase as the body's need increases. Women, for example - who need to replenish iron lost in menstruation - absorb a greater percentage of iron compared to men.

Fast Fact

More women die each year as a result of hip fractures than from breast and ovarian cancer combined.

For both men and women, peak bone density is achieved during late adolescence. Around 35 years of age, bones begin to thin for both sexes. This process accelerates for women when estrogen levels drop at menopause. Women lose about one-third of their bone mass during their lifetimes while men lose about one-fifth. The more bone mass one develops as an adolescent, the more protected one will be from the inevitable loss that happens as you get older.

In a recent study of adolescent girls, raising calcium intake with supplements from 80% of the current recommended dietary allowance to 110% increased bone mass by more than 1% per year during adolescent growth. In another study, of men and women ages 50 to 79, those in the top third in terms of calcium consumption suffered 60% fewer hip fractures over the next 14 years than the others. Calcium is essential throughout life.

Here's a red flag for caffeine lovers - too much caffeine can reduce your calcium levels. A recent Harvard University study of 84,000 middle-aged women found that those who drank more than four cups of coffee a day were three times more likely to suffer from hip fractures than women who had little or no caffeine.

Zinc

Zinc has amazing healing properties and forms part of more than 300 enzymes needed to repair wounds. Zinc helps maintain fertility in adults and growth in children. It also synthesizes protein, helps cells reproduce, preserves vision, boosts immunity and protects against free radicals, just to name some of the most important functions. Zinc ointment is often topically applied to heal skin abrasions and is also used to soothe a baby's skin.

At an international conference in Stockholm held in June of 2000, researchers described experiments which indicate that zinc supplements enhance growth and weight gain and reduce the risk of diarrhea in children. Zinc also reduces the incidence of pneumonia and possibly malaria as well as the risk of complications in pregnancy.

While it's great to know the many functions zinc performs, it's alarming to realize that an estimated 48% of the globe's population don't get enough zinc. Zinc deficiencies are common in HIV patients. Even a small deficiency in this critical mineral can have a huge effect.

Health Tip

Calcium is best absorbed in an acidic environment - look for a calcium supplement that contains betaine hydrochloride or hydrochloric acid.

Fast Fact

There are 70 known protein-synthesizing enzymes that can't function without zinc.

Older people are particularly vulnerable to a lack of zinc which may affect their eyesight as well as their memory. Zinc stimulates an enzyme critical in the retinal cells. Without zinc, the cells may become abnormal, resulting in macular degeneration - a common cause of blindness in elderly people.

As for memory, Dr. Harold Sandstead, a zinc expert at the University of Texas Medical Branch in Galveston found that otherwise healthy people, deprived of zinc did poorly on memory and concentration tests. The idea that fish is brain food may have an element of truth since it contains zinc - the brain booster!

Selenium

Selenium is a powerful antioxidant mineral being tested in exciting and groundbreaking studies around the world for its anticancer and heart disease prevention properties.

A study conducted by Dr. Larry Clark, published in the *Journal of the American Medical Association (JAMA)* created quite a stir when it showed that over 1,300 people given 200 mcg of yeast-based selenium per day for 4.5 years had a 50% drop in the cancer death rate compared to the placebo rate. Another study compared men who consumed the most selenium to men with the lowest levels and found that those who consumed the most had 65% fewer cases of advanced prostate cancer than the other men tested.

The Selenium and Vitamin E Cancer Prevention Trial (SELECT), sponsored by the National Cancer Institute and covering the next ten to fifteen years, is currently investigating 32,000 men to look at the role of vitamin E and selenium in the prevention of prostate cancer. It is anticipated that these extensive long-term tests will confirm what other studies have found: that selenium is associated with a significantly reduced risk of prostate cancer.

Selenium is also essential for healthy immune functioning. Supplements have also reduced cases of viral hepatitis in selenium-deficient populations. Even in a non-deficient population of elderly people, selenium supplementation has been found to stimulate the activity of white blood cells - the primary components of the immune system. Selenium also activates thyroid hormones. In a double-blind trial, selenium supplementation of infertile men improved the motility of sperm cells and increased the chance of conception.

Your body can best use selenium when it's in an organically bound yeast-based form - this way, even in high doses, it's not toxic.

Did You Know...

Drinking too many sodas will lead to high levels of phosphorous which can create an imbalance of calcium and magnesium and weaken bone strength.

Fast Fact

Dr. Larry Clark's research recommends 200 mcg of selenium. To get this from diet alone, a person would have to consume over one pound of shrimp (approximately 85 medium sized shrimp) per day.

Magnesium

Magnesium is involved in more than 300 enzymatic reactions in the body. Research on magnesium's benefits dates to the early 1930's but it has recently made a comeback. At the beginning to the century, most Americans got about 1,200 milligrams of magnesium a day in their diet, while today the

Did You Know...

Selenium improves the immune system's "memory" and its ability to quickly make more anti-body-producing cells in response to new infections.

minimum RDA is only 400 mg - and not all of us get that. A recent survey suggests that 72% of adult North Americans aren't meeting the RDA for magnesium.

Our bodies need magnesium more than ever today since polluted air and water can interfere with its proper functioning. Promising research into the connections between magnesium and heart disease cause health experts to now believe that magnesium deficiency can be linked to hardening of the arteries and high blood pressure.

Do you associate heart attacks with clogged arteries? Did you know that 25% of heart attacks occur in people with healthy arteries that are not clogged with fats? The link in these cases seems to be a magnesium deficiency. In fact, treatment with intravenous magnesium improves the survival rate of patients who've just had a heart attack.

Recently, magnesium has been investigated in terms of reducing symptoms of pre-menstrual syndrome. Women who generally suffer from headaches, intense cramps and fatigue were deficient in magnesium and these symptoms were alleviated by magnesium supplements.

Conclusion

Evidence that we need minerals not only for basic survival, but also for optimal health and disease prevention is indisputable. It is also clear that we are not getting adequate amounts of these vital nutrients from our diets anymore. Agricultural practices and soil erosion are taking minerals out of our soil and the foods we eat. A quality supplement, taken with a meal, will ensure that you are providing your body with adequate levels of dietary minerals.

Take Action Today

1. Make sure your multivitamin & mineral supplement contains a full complement of both macro and micro minerals.

2. Take your vitamin and mineral supplement with food containing protein to maximize absorption.

3. Along with your multi-vitamin and mineral supplement, take additional calcium and organically bound selenium.

Table 5-1: Mineral Chart

Mineral	Role in the Body	Sources	Health Conditions Supported or Focus of Current Research	RDA Women	RDA Men	Antioxidant Properties
Calcium	Essential for developing and maintaining healthy bones and teeth. Assists in blood clotting, muscle contraction, nerve transmission. Reduces risk of osteoporosis.	Dairy products, green leafy vegetables, canned fish, tofu.	Osteoporosis, High blood pressure, High cholesterol	800 mg	800 mg	
Magnesium	Activates nearly 100 enzymes and helps nerves and muscles function.	Green vegetables, legumes, cereal, fish, and whole bran.	Heart Health, Diabetes, Migraine headaches, ADD, Osteoporosis	350 mg	280 mg	
Potassium	Maintaining fluid balance.	Spinach, brussel sprouts, bananas, potatoes, tomatoes, orange juice, cantaloupe.	High blood pressure, Cardiovascular disease	--	--	
Iron	Needed for red blood cell formation and function.	Liver, meats, green leafy vegetables, enriched breads and cereals.	Anemia, Canker sores, HIV support, Infertility (female)	15 mg	10mg	
Zinc	Essential part of more than 100 enzymes involved in digestion, metabolism, reproduction and wound healing.	Meat, liver, poultry, fish, oysters, other seafood, whole grains, eggs.	Common cold/sore throat, Wilson's disease, Wound healing, Crohn's disease, HIV support, Infection Immune function, Macular degeneration	12 mg	15mg	
Iodine	Helps regulate, growth, development, metabolism. Necessary for normal thyroid function.	Iodized salt, saltwater fish, dairy products, white bread.	Goiter, hypothyroidism	150 mcg	150mcg	

Mineral	Role in the Body	Sources	Health Conditions Supported or Focus of Current Research	RDA Women	RDA Men	Antioxidant Properties
Selenium	Necessary for normal growth, development, use of iodine in thyroid function. May reduce risk of certain cancers.	Whole grains, fish, seafood, liver, meats, eggs.	Cancer, Asthma, Atherosclerosis, Infections, HIV support, Macular Degeneration, Rheumatoid Arthritis	55 mcg	70 mcg	
Copper	Involved in iron metabolism, nervous system function, bone health, synthesis of proteins. Plays a role in pigmentation of skin, hair, eyes.	Liver, seafood, nuts, seeds.	High cholesterol, Benign Prostatic Hyperplasia, Osteoporosis, Rheumatoid Arthritis	0.9mg *	0.9 mg *	
Manganese	Necessary for normal development of skeletal and connective tissues. Involved in metabolism of carbohydrates.	Whole grains, cereals.	Hypoglycemia, Osteoporosis, Minor injuries	2.3 mg *	2.3 mg *	✓
Chromium	Normal glucose metabolism.	Egg yolks, whole grains, pork.	Diabetes, High cholesterol, Hypoglycemia, Athletic performance, Weight loss, Depression	35 mcg*	35 mcg *	✓
Molybdenum	Needed for metabolism of DNA and RNA.	Milk, beans, breads, cereals.	Asthma	45 mcg*	45 mcg*	

*No RDA for these nutrients, value given is the Daily Reference Intake as per recommendation of the Food and Nutrition Board of the Institute of Medicine

+Nutrient Recommendations will vary by country.

CHAPTER 6

The Healing Power of Herbs

Did You Know...

An ancient, 60,000 year-old grave in Iraq contained a bouquet of common remedial herbs including milk thistle, yarrow and mallow.

One of the first modern drugs to be isolated from a plant was morphine, first identified in 1803 by scientist Friedrich Serturner. He extracted white crystals from crude opium poppy.

Herbs have been known and used for their healing powers for centuries. The next time you pop a piece of licorice in your mouth, consider that you've just joined forces with one of the earliest cultures on earth. The Sumerians (one of the world's first civilizations) were very familiar with medicinal herbs such as licorice and thyme, according to ancient clay tablets that date around 4000 BC.

A Chinese text called the Pen Tsao, which dates to 3000 BC, contained some 1,000 herbal formulas which had likely been around for thousands of years before that. In Egypt, records that date to 1700 BC show that herbs such as juniper and garlic were known and used since 4000 BC. Egyptians also knew about the wonderful properties of chamomile. Women like Cleopatra crushed the petals of the flower to beautify and protect their skin from harsh dry weather. These ancient cultures depended on herbs to maintain their health and beauty. What did they know that we don't? Plenty!

Traditionally, many cultures have used and still use herbs to effectively maintain health as well as to heal ailments as diverse as eye infections, stomach aches, impotence and headaches. In fact, one of the first things the Pilgrims did when they got off the boat in Plymouth, Massachusetts in 1630 was to transplant the herbal seedlings they'd lovingly transported across the Atlantic. They also soon began to explore the native North American healing plants such as cascara sagrada and goldenseal, adding them to their repertoire.

Health Tip

Regular use of ginseng has been shown to boost the level of white blood cells - a sign of increased immune system functioning.

Fast Fact

Europe's oldest surviving writing about herbs dates from the first half of the 10th century and includes remedies sent by the patriarch of Jerusalem to the King.

The word botanical has encompassed many different things including roots, leaves, barks and berries. You'll find the term herb and botanical are often used interchangeably. Today, herbs are generally defined as a plant, or part of a plant valued for its medicinal, savory, or aromatic qualities.

Herbs contain nutrients that are often not found in any other foods we eat. While our ancestors used to consume herbs as part of their regular diet, we rarely find ourselves 'chewing on a piece of bark' - nor would we want to. Still, the nutrients found in botanicals are unique and of great value to our health. An herbal supplement is our modern day alternative.

Herbal medicine has now come out of the realm of folklore and underground into mainstream medical schools around the world where medicinal botanical properties are being studied and prescribed. Germany is one country leading the way. In emergency rooms in Germany, milk thistle is routinely used intravenously to preserve the liver function of patients suffering from alcohol poisoning or drug overdoses. This wonderful, non-toxic way of approaching medicine is something all countries should be doing. Germany is also the only country in the world where hypericum, the active ingredient in St. John's Wort, is clinically approved for use and doctors prescribe more than 66 million doses annually for psychological complaints. German doctors prescribe St. John's Wort about 20 times more often than Prozac, which is one of the most widely prescribed pharmaceutical antidepressants in North America.

Fast Fact

30-40% of all medical doctors in France and Germany rely on herbal preparations as their primary medicines.

While countries such as China, Japan, Korea, France, and Germany are pre-scribing herbal remedies for a wide variety of complaints, in North America, herbs are still being viewed with suspicion by the medical community and are often bypassed in favour of treating illnesses with either drugs or surgery.

Patients are beginning to question the wisdom of the modern approach to med-icine involving drugs and surgery and request a less invasive method of main-taining and regaining health. The marketplace is already responding to these popular demands and herbal remedies are now widely available. They're still not completely accepted though, particularly by the medical profession and the drug industry.

One problem is that herbal remedies are not as high profit as drugs. A drug can be patented which gives the manufacturing company exclusive rights to it while herbs are readily available to most consumers and are rarely patent-ed. If a company invests millions of dollars in researching and proving the effects of a certain herb, another company, who hasn't paid for the research, can put the herb on the market at a lower price. For the first company, it's a losing proposition.

Since there are not large profits involved, herbal companies don't court the doctors the way pharmaceutical companies do. The result is a bias toward treating illnesses with drugs rather than gently coaxing the body into healing itself with herbal remedies, or preventing illness in the first place.

While pharmaceuticals and modern medicine are definitely beneficial and required under certain circumstances, we seem to have invested far too much in trying to fix health problems, rather than in prevention. Our health-care sys-tem has become a crisis or chronic illness management system. When you consider the growing number of illnesses that are managed, such as cancer, asthma, heart condition, multiple sclerosis, arthritis, etc., rather than prevent-ed, you realize that the modern health system is in big trouble.

Did You Know...

Historically, herbs were chosen based on their shape in relation to the body. For example, liver-shaped leaves were used to cure liver ailments; yel-low herbs were used to treat jaun-dice, red herbs for blood problems, etc. Research is now beginning to validate many of these theories.

Fast Fact

Approximately 95% of the trillion dollars the United States spends on health goes to direct health servic-es, while only 5% is set aside for preventive medicine.

Did You Know...

Herbs are often taken in blended preparations containing multiple botanicals. These herbs work together to produce a greater benefit, known as the synergistic effect.

Today, we seem to think it's perfectly fine to take drugs for the rest of our lives that treat the symptoms rather than the cause of a disease. Unlike herbs, drugs not only cost a lot, they can extract a high cost from our bodies as well. Masking symptoms without addressing the root cause of an illness can be dangerous since symptoms are the body's way of signaling to us that all is not well.

There is a different way of looking at health and wellness, called holistic healing that is attracting more attention. The premise behind holistic healing is basically that, under optimal nutritional and lifestyle conditions, your body has the ability to heal itself. If the body is under too much stress, holistic medicine incorporating herbs can help the body regain its balance so it can then do what it was designed to do - heal. A holistic approach to healing considers all aspects of life including nutritional intake, lifestyle, current health status, inherited weaknesses and emotional health. Many herbalists believe that mind, body and soul are interconnected and one part cannot be treated without considering the whole.

It seems modern medicine is recognizing this truth and coming full circle, back to its roots. The latest cancer and AIDS experimental trials involve stimulating and boosting the body's immune system so that the body can heal itself! It's not such a radical thought after all.

Fast Fact

Properly researched, regulated, prescribed and used drugs are the fourth most common cause of death in North America - but they are rarely reported.

Plants to Pharmaceuticals

Did you realize that more than 25% of all prescription drugs contain active ingredients that come from plants? Many over-the-counter remedies are made from plant compounds as well.

White willow bark is the original source of salicyn which forms the basis for aspirin. Salicyn was artificially synthesized for the first time in 1852. Later, modifications were made to make it less irritating to the stomach and in 1899, an acetylsalicylic acid product called aspirin was launched by a famous drug company.

Fast Fact

Rainforests once covered 14% of the earth's land surface; now they cover a mere 6% and experts estimate that the last remaining rainforests could be consumed in less than 40 years. Only 1% of the plant species found in the rainforest have been examined by scientists.

Did You Know...

Herbs and spices were not only used for medicinal purposes long before they became culinary seasonings, they were also often used for currency.

Long before any of this happened, of course, white willow bark was used to combat many general aches and pains. Mention of white willow bark can be found in ancient Egyptian, Assyrian and Greek manuscripts and this potent herb was used to treat pain and fever by ancient physicians Galen, Hippocrates and Dioscorides. Native American Indians used it for headaches, fever, sore muscles, rheumatism and chills. We've gone from using herbal remedies to creating drugs out of herbs and are now moving back to using herbs in their pure form again.

Increasing Popularity of Herbs

According to the Nutrition Business Journal, ancient herbal remedies are making a strong comeback with more than US$17 billion being spent on botanicals world-wide. Europe is the world's largest market for herbal medicine products, with retail sales amounting to US$6.9 billion in recent years. The U.S. is not too far behind with more than US$4.1 billion worth of herbal medicines purchased in the year 2001.

Fast Fact

The World Health Organization estimated, in 1985, that roughly 80% of the world's population relies on traditional medicines, including herbs, for primary health care needs.

You may however, find yourself confused when making a purchase. There's such a variety of makes and models of herbal remedies with each one claiming to be exactly what you need. How can you choose what's best for you and what provides the best value?

Let me help you sort through the confusion. Herbal preparations can be found in four basic forms - extracts, tinctures, decoctions or teas, all of which can be very effective providing quality product is chosen.

Extract can be either in a solid or a liquid form. The active ingredients are concentrated by low temperature distillation so that the chemical nature of the extract is not altered. Or the extract can be made by mixing the herb with an alcohol or water solvent. The solid extracts are made by evaporation.

Health Tip

Garlic can help reduce blood pressure and cholesterol - use it daily

Tinctures are typically made by using an alcohol and water mixture as the solvent. The herb is soaked in the solvent for a specified amount of time, depending on the herb. The solution is then pressed out, yielding the tincture.

Decoctions are made by leaving a plant in water for a certain amount of time before removing it. This disperses the active ingredients in the water.

Teas are made by boiling the herb in water.

Active Ingredients in Botanicals

Active ingredients provide the health benefits in botanicals and each herb has its own particular active ingredients, such as ginsenosides in ginseng, cascarosides in cascara bark and flavonoids in licorice root, to name just a few. The concentration of active ingredients found in an herb will vary according to growing conditions, soil conditions, how they've been harvested and preserved as well as how long they've been in storage.

If you grow and harvest fresh herbs yourself to use in salads or teas, you have control over the quality. In the retail store, it's a much different story. You're faced with a multitude of choices and not enough information to make an informed decision. All the bottles facing you contain the same herb...but herbs without a high level of active ingredients are like yogurt without an active culture. In other words, useless!

Standardization

Fortunately, recent advances in extraction processes, coupled with improved analytical methods, have ensured that companies who use standardized methods of extracting and measuring the active ingredients have the highest level of quality control.

Standardization is the ability to accurately measure the active ingredient in each botanical. For example, in the case of ginseng, the active ingredient ginsenosides would be the compound measured and standardized to a specific concentration, to ensure a quality product.

So no matter what form the herb is in or how it's been processed, standardization guarantees that the active botanical ingredient is at the specified level. In other words, only buy herbs from a company you know and trust.

Safety of Herbs versus Prescription Drugs

While the popularity of herbs has grown by leaps and bounds around the world, so has the rise of a backlash that warns of the dangers of taking 'untested' herbs. I'd say anything that's been used for thousands of years has a pretty good track record. Of course, you have to be cautious when taking anything and use good judgment, but generally herbs when taken correctly are very safe.

We tend to put trust in the safety of drugs, yet a recent study in the *Journal of the American Medical Association (JAMA)* found that in a one-year period, more than two million hospitalized patients who took prescription drugs according to directions suffered serious reactions, and more than 106,000 people died as a result.

On the other hand, the herbal dietary supplements that often get such a negative reaction from the media have averaged fewer than five confirmed deaths per year over the past 25 years in the U.S., and most of these were related to self-diagnosis and taking amounts much higher then the manufacturers suggested dosage. Twice the dose does not give twice the benefit - and in fact, can be dangerous!

How Botanicals Help Fight Body Pollution

Botanicals taken on a regular basis can provide unique nutrients that help keep the body in top condition. When fighting body pollution, certain specific bodily systems require additional support. Many botanicals target these systems specifically. Let's take a look at a few in detail.

Immune System

Certain herbs, such as astragalus, which has been used in China as an immune booster for 400 years, directly assist the immune system. Reishi mushroom, Siberian ginseng and licorice root also work to stimulate and support the immune system.

Did You Know...

Buying standardized herbal products is the only way to ensure you are getting a guaranteed level of active ingredients.

Herbs are often used to correct underlying imbalances rather than just to give temporary relief. It is for this reason that the effects of herbal remedies can sometimes take longer to become apparent.

Health
Tip

Herbal extracts generally contain very tiny amounts of vitamins and minerals and do not take the place of a vitamin and mineral supplement - use both for optimal health.

Antioxidant System

Other botanicals such as German chamomile, Chinese pearl barley and licorice root act as antioxidants and fight against free radical damage. German chamomile, with particularly potent flavonoids has documented antioxidant properties known to protect skin from the ravages of free radicals induced by pollution, overexposure to the sun, poor diet or a host of other disease-causing agents.

Digestive System

Ginger root, chicory and capsicum all help support the digestive system. Ancient Greeks used to wrap ginger in bread to aid with digestion and today ginger tea is often used to sooth a nauseous stomach.

Energy System

Several botanicals are thought of as health tonics or energy boosters. Tonics are used to enhance general health and can be safely taken for a long period of time. Rose hips, Siberian ginseng, reishi mushroom and schisandra berry are some of the herbs considered tonics.

Detoxification System

Herbs act as excellent detoxifiers. Aloe vera, schisandra berry, dandelion root and milk thistle are all herbs that help to cleanse the systems of the body. As we are exposed to more and more body pollution, our bodies need assistance in cleansing the by-products of this pollution.

Conclusion

Herbs have been used around the world for thousands of years as a natural way to support the body. Herbs are basically nature's way of allowing us to treat ourselves with unique nutrients the way the earth intended. Rarely do we eat foods today that contain these beneficial nutrients, however with the negative effects of body pollution affecting us all, we may need them more than ever. A daily herbal supplement is an excellent way to provide your body with these vital nutrients.

Take Action Today

1. *Use herbs daily to support and strengthen the body in the fight against body pollution.*

2. *Whenever possible, use standardized herbal supplements to ensure a consistent level of active compounds.*

3. *Refer to the enclosed chart to use specific herbs for related health issues.*

Table 6-1: Herb Chart

Herb	Active Ingredients	Action in Body	Focus of Current Research/ Traditional Use	Antioxidant Activity
Alfalfa	Saponin Glycosides	Mild diuretic, tonic	High cholesterol, Menopause, Poor appetite, Arthritis, Diabetes	
Aloe Vera	Anthraquinone Glycosides, Polysaccharides	General tonic, Detoxifier, Immune Function	Chrone's disease, Diabetes, Peptic ulcers, Psoriasis, Wound healing, Immune support	
Astragalus	Flavonoids, Polysaccharides, Triterpene glycosides	Immune function, Tonic, Antiviral, Antioxidant	Common cold/infection, Immune support, Diabetes, AIDS, Hepatitis, Heart attack	✓
Bee Pollen	Vitamins Minerals	Anti-infectant, Anti-allergic, Liver support, Provides energy	Cancer risk reduction, Rheumatoid Arthritis, Hay Fever	
Bladderwrack	Phenolic compounds, Mucopolysaccharides	Supports metabolism, Antioxidant	Weight management	✓
Boswellia	Boswellic Acid	Digestive aid	Stress, Anxiety	
Capsicum	Capsaicin	Circulatory stimulant, Tonic, Anti-inflammatory, Analgesic	Diabetes, Arthritis, Psoriasis	
Cascara Bark	Cascarosides	Mild laxative, Tonic	Constipation	
Celery Seed	Glycosides Flavonoids	Digestive aid, Muscle relaxant, Anti-inflammatory	Arthritis, Gout, Bronchitis, Blood pressure	✓
Chicory Root	Inulin, Coumarin Glycosides	Tonic, Digestive aid	Digestive problems, Liver/gallbladder ailments	
Chinese Pearl Barley	Coixol, Coixans	Antioxidant, Anti-inflammatory, Tonic	Painful joints, Rheumatism, Swelling	✓
Citrus Aurantium	Synephrine	Supports metabolism, Appetite suppressant	Weight management	✓
Couch Grass	Polysaccharides, Volatile Oils	Mild diuretic, Cleanser	Urinary tract infections, Gout	
Dandelion Root	Triterpenes, Phenolic compounds, Carotenoids	Tonic, Mild diuretic, Liver support, Blood purifier	Constipation, Gallstones, Indigestion, heartburn	✓

Herb	Active Ingredients	Action in Body	*Focus of Current Research/* *Traditional Use*	*Antioxidant* *Activity*
Fenugreek	Saponins, Flavonoids	Digestive aid, Tonic, Expectorant, Antioxidant	Diabetes, High triglycerides, Constipation, Atherosclerosis, Arthritis, Bronchitis, High cholesterol	✓
German Chamomile	Flavonoids, Volatile oils	Anti-inflammatory, Mild sedative, Tonic, Antioxidant	Colic, Eczema, Gingivitis (periodontal disease), Wound healing, Irritable bowel syndrome	✓
Ginger Root	Volatile Oils, Gingerols	Digestive aid, Anti inflammatory, Anti-nausea, Detoxicant	Nausea, Indigestion, Atherosclerosis, Migraine headaches, Rheumatoid arthritis	
Juniper Berry	Volatile Oils, Flavonoids, Sterols, Catechins	Mild diuretic, Anti-inflammatory, Antioxidant, Digestive aid	Edema (water retention), Indigestion, Kidney and bladder infection, Gout, Cancer protection, Blood pressure	✓
Lemon Balm	Volatile Oils, Flavonoids, Phenolic Acids	Digestive aid, Calming effect, Antioxidant	Indigestion, Heartburn, Insomnia	✓
Licorice Root	Flavonoids	Antioxidant, Detoxicant, Expectorant	Asthma, Chronic fatigue, Bronchitis, HIV support	✓
Parsley	Volatile Oils, Coumarins Flavonoids	Digestive Aid, Mild diuretic, Antioxidant, Anti-inflammatory	Traditional seasoning	✓
Passion Flower	Flavonoids, Volatile Oils	Anti-anxiety, Antioxidant	Anxiety, Insomnia, Pain	✓
Phaseolus Vulgaris (White Kidney Bean Extract)	Glycoproteins	Digestive aid, Starch neutralizer	Weight management	
Pipsissewa	Hydroquinones, Flavonoids	Tonic, Astringent, Kidney support, Antioxidant	Inflammation, Urinary tract infection	✓
Reishi Mushroom	Sterols, Coumarin, Polysaccharides	Immune function	Blood pressure, High cholesterol, Immune support, Cardiovascular disease	
Rose Hip	Flavanoids, Vitamins	Astringent, Diuretic, Tonic	Blood purifier, Infections	✓
Sarsaparilla	Saponins	Anti-inflammatory, Tonic, Detoxicant, Liver protectant	Psoriasis, Rheumatoid arthritis, Gout	

Table 6-1: Herb Chart

Herb	Active Ingredients	Action in Body	Focus of Current Research/ Traditional Use	Antioxidant Activity
Schisandra Berry	Lignans	Immune function, Liver support, Activation of antioxidant enzymes, Tonic, Antioxidant	Common cold/sore throat, Fatigue, Hepatitis, Infection, Liver support, Stress	✓
Siberian Ginseng	Eleutherosides, Polysaccharides	Immune function, Energy, Adaptogen	Fatigue, Common cold, Fybromyalgia, Infection, Diabetes	
Tamarind	Volatile Oils	Anti-inflammatory, Digestive aid, Analgesic	Traditional spice	
Thyme	Volatile Oils, Flavonoids	Anti-tussive, Expectorant, Antioxidant	Bronchitis, Cough, Indigestion	✓
Turmeric	Curcuminoids, Volatile Oils	Antioxidant, Anti-inflammatory, Liver protectant	Traditional spice	✓
Uva Ursi	Hydroquinones, Flavonoids	Mild diuretic, Antioxidant	Weight management, Urinary tract infection	✓
Yerba Mate	Mateine	Metabolic enhancer, Mild diuretic	Weight management	

CHAPTER

The Phenomenal Power of Phytonutrients

Did You Know...

Brightly coloured fruits and vegetables such as those that are yellow, orange, red, green, blue and purple - generally contain the most phytonutrients.

Since you may not be aware of the amazing benefits that phytonutrients provide, let me introduce you to these underappreciated allies in the fight for good health - with the hope that you may soon become well acquainted! The truth is, what you don't know can hurt you.

In my opinion, phytonutrients are one of nature's strongest partners in the battle against body pollution. You may also see them being called phytochemicals, as the terms are often used interchangeably. If you want to be vibrantly healthy, you'll need to know all about them and the great benefits they provide. It's a very worthwhile education! The word 'phyto' means plant in Greek and the word phytonutrient refers to a multitude of beneficial chemical compounds naturally found in plant foods. There are literally thousands of different individual phytonutrients many of which you may already know - carotenoids, bioflavonoids, lycopene, and sulforaphane to name a few.

Nature clearly has a master plan in place that we're just beginning to figure out since phytonutrients are most often found in plants that we eat on a regular basis - generally speaking, fruits, vegetables, nuts and grains, etc. - and are often what give these foods their particular colours and flavour. Nutritionists frequently advise clients to eat a wide variety of fruits and vegetables so that they benefit from the different phytonutrients found in these foods.

Health
Tip

All fruits and vegetables are most nutritious when served raw. The best cooking method is steaming with very little water.

Fast Fact

An orange has more than 170 phytonutrients in its skin, oil, pulp, flesh and juice which may protect your health.

Although phytonutrients have been around forever, they have only recently been 'discovered'. This discovery ranks in importance with that of vitamins. Phytonutrient armies protect plants from disease, injuries, insects, poisons, pollutants, drought, excessive heat and ultraviolet rays. They may also serve as antioxidants. In a sense, they protect the plants from their own sources of body pollution. Recent research suggests they perform the same function for humans.

Phytonutrients may also enhance immune response and cell-to-cell communication, which allows your body's built-in defenses to work more efficiently. They are true multi-taskers and work in the body to help regulate hormones, repair DNA damage caused by smoking and many sources of body pollution, as well as detoxify carcinogens by working with the body's enzymes.

More importantly, there is growing scientific consensus that these nutritional powerhouses play a crucial role in the prevention of chronic degenerative diseases including many cancers. Phytonutrients have also been linked to lowering cholesterol, reducing blood pressure, detoxifying blood and relieving allergies.

While these potent agents are an extra element in preserving health, they're not directly linked to our survival the same way that carbohydrates, fats, proteins, vitamins, minerals and water are, simply because we can survive without them. Survival is one thing, thriving is another. Phytonutrients are essential to thriving and maintaining optimum health. If your definition of health includes the absence of disease, then you'll realize their true importance.

Fast Fact

People who eat 5 or more servings of fruits and vegetables every day have half the risk of developing cancer as those who eat only one or two servings per day.

As research on these amazing nutrients is still in its infancy, there is no RDA (Recommended Dietary Allowance) associated with them - as of this writing. This picture is changing on a daily basis, as researchers uncover an increasingly long list of benefits they provide. It is quite possible that one day they'll be classified as essential nutrients, since evidence is steadily growing to show that getting the right balance of phytonutrients on a daily basis is indeed vital to maintaining excellent health.

Nutritionists talk about a balanced diet for good reason. Many of the essential nutrients your body depends on work best in combination. The concept of synergy - meaning the whole is worth more than the sum of its parts, can be used here. Flavonoids and carotenoids have more powerful health-promoting properties when eaten together in the same food. Every one of the hundreds (perhaps thousands) of phytonutrients is a team player and works best in conjunction with other nutrients. Certain vitamins and minerals can also enhance the effectiveness of phytonutrients. For example, using the mineral selenium with phytonutrients can provide optimal antioxidant cellular protection.

Since each class of phytonutrients affects cellular well-being in different ways, the best way to take full advantage of the best medicine nature has to offer is to eat a variety of these compounds. One phytonutrient may neutralize a carcinogen to keep it from attaching onto a cell, another may whisk carcinogens out of the cells, another may handcuff free radicals so they don't roam free in the body, and others stimulate the body's own enzymes to break up potential cancer-causing chemicals. You'll want the soldiers in this army to work in a troop rather than alone so they can defend you better. Nature knows best, so avail yourself of nature's bounty as scientists scramble to do the research. Your glowing health will give you all the evidence you need that a wide variety of phytonutrients can protect your health.

Did You Know...

Women who develop breast cancer tend to have blood levels of carotenoids as much as 21% lower than those of healthy women.

Eating Your Fruits and Vegetables

The prestigious National Academy of Sciences would applaud your choice to increase fruits and vegetables on a daily basis. They emphasized the importance of including fruits and vegetables in one's daily diet in a landmark report released back in 1982. The value of citrus fruits, carotene-rich fruits and cruciferous vegetables such as broccoli, cabbage and cauliflower for reducing cancer risk was specifically highlighted. Since this ground-breaking study, evidence has been piling up.

Health Tip

The nutrients in fruits and vegetables are often concentrated just below the skin - avoid peeling whenever possible.

Fast Fact

Surveys done by the National Research Council indicates that only 10% of the US population consumes five serving of fruits and vegetables per day.

In 1989, the same Academy stressed again the importance of fruits and vegetables for reducing the risk of both cancer and heart disease and recommended five or more servings of fruits and vegetables daily. In 1992, the 5 A Day For Better Health program was launched by the National Cancer Institute. Since then, health agencies all over the world have joined the chorus. Eat more fruits and vegetables! And remember, five is the minimum.

There's been a compelling case made for increasing our consumption of fresh fruits and vegetables but it seems we're not listening. At present, the average adult in some Asian countries eats about one serving of vegetables and slightly less than one serving of fruit a day. Eighty percent of U.S. children and adolescents don't eat the recommended servings.

If you know you should eat more fruits and vegetables but just aren't motivated, here's a very persuasive argument for changing your ways: those who eat the least amount of fruits and vegetables have roughly twice the cancer rate for most types of cancer (lung, larynx, oral cavity, esophagus, stomach, colorectal, bladder, pancreas, cervix and ovarian).

You might think that an orange for breakfast or an apple at lunchtime or some green pepper in your spaghetti sauce and a serving of french fries fit the bill. Not by a long shot! What I'd like to impress on you is that you need quantity, quality and variety. That variety needs to change on a daily basis if you really want to get the maximum benefits.

Below is a list that illustrates how powerful an ally phytonutrients are in protecting us from body pollution and chronic disease.

Today we know that phytonutrients have these functions:

• Reduce the risk of cardiovascular disease by reversing high cholesterol and triglycerides and helping to reduce free radical damage, platelet stickiness and degeneration of blood vessel walls.

• Reduce cancer risk by activating the body's defense mechanisms and blocking the action of carcinogens.

• Detoxify cancer promoters and free radical inducers.

• Modify hormone levels, reduce the risk of cancers from excess hormone action.

• Act as potent antioxidants.

• Influence metabolic enzymes to benefit the entire body.

• Boost immune response by activating different classes of immune-system components.

• Inhibit bacterial, viral, fungal and parasitic attack.

• Protect the body's structural components.

That's an impressive list! But just in case you're not completely motivated to increase the fruits and vegetables in your daily diet, let's look at the current research.

Fruit and Vegetable Research

• The men and women who eat the most fruits and vegetables are 20% less likely to have heart disease, according to recent research at Harvard University. Adding just one fruit or vegetable a day cuts heart disease risk by 4%.

• In a recent Dutch study of male smokers, those who ate the most fruit were only half as likely to die of lung cancer as those who ate the least.

• Women who ate 2 1/2 servings of fruits and vegetables daily were 65% less likely to have colorectal cancer than women who ate 1 1/2 servings, according to Swedish research.

• Eating more fruits and vegetables is more effective at combating excess weight than eating less high-fat, high-sugar food, according to recent research at the State University of New York, Buffalo.

• Women who eat at least five daily servings of fruits and vegetables reduce their risk of diabetes by 40% compared women who don't, according to a study by the federal Centers for Disease Control and Prevention.

If you double the amount of fruits and vegetables that you eat, you'll increase the

Did You Know...

Lycopene is better absorbed by the body after it has been heated during processing - good examples are tomato sauce and ketchup.

antioxidant power of your blood between 13 and 25 percent. Now that's incentive! The vitamins, minerals and phytonutrients contained in these rich foods work together to help you fight body pollution.

Here are some of the powerful phytonutrients and how they work in the body. You'll find a more detailed list in the phytonutrient chart at the end of this chapter.

Lycopene

Lycopene is what gives tomatoes, watermelons, grapefruits and papaya their red colour. It is a pigment synthesized by some plants and animals to protect them from the sun, and evolved as a weapon against certain types of free radicals. In one study, lycopene proved even more effective in neutralizing free radicals than vitamin E.

Fast Fact

Initially cultivated by the Aztecs, tomatoes started out yellow. Through breeding efforts over the centuries, most now ripen into a deep, lycopene-rich red.

Italians have a very low incidence of cancer of the digestive tract and it's thought that this is because they eat a lot of tomato sauce. Studies have shown that lycopene can considerably reduce the risk of cancer.

One six-year-study by Harvard Medical School and Harvard School of Public Health looked at the diets of more than 47,000 men from all over the world. They evaluated 46 fruits and vegetables and discovered only tomato products (which contain large quantities of lycopene) reduce prostate cancer risk. As consumption of tomato products increased, levels of lycopene in the blood rose and the risk for prostate cancer decreased. The study also showed that the heat processing of tomatoes and tomato products increases lycopene's effectiveness. Doctors concluded that eating tomatoes, tomato sauce or pizza more than twice a week as opposed to never could lead to a 21-34% reduction in the incidence of prostate cancer.

Up until now, researchers speculated that the Mediterranean diet was associated with a reduced risk of cancer because of olive oil's health benefits but now they think it may be due to lycopene. Because tomatoes and olives are so intertwined in the diet, it's hard to separate out the effects each one has on health.

Exciting new research now underway links lycopene to a reduced risk of macular degeneration, cardiovascular disease and cancers of the lung, bladder, cervix and skin. Studies at both the University of Toronto and the American Health Foundation will focus on lycopene's role in fighting against cancers of the digestive tract, breast and prostate. It seems lycopene has more than one cancer-fighting characteristic - it has antioxidant properties and also appears to modulate immunity, help keep cancer tumors under control and regulate hormones.

Sulforaphane

Sulforaphane, one of the most studied phytonutrients, boosts the immune system's capacity for detoxifying carcinogens. Vegetables like broccoli taste a little bitter in part because of sulfuric compounds and this is why our children may complain about eating them! This is one occasion when parents know best because within hours of eating, sulforaphane enters the bloodstream where it triggers cancer-fighting elements of the immune system by activating a group of proteins called phase 2 enzymes. These enzymes then jump into action and attach the carcinogen to a molecule that quickly destroys and removes it. That battle has been won!

Sulforaphane may also prevent breast cancer. In a study at John Hopkins Medical Institution, scientists added sulforaphane to human cells grown in a lab dish and found that it increased the effectiveness of cancer-fighting enzymes. The same scientists injected rats with a known carcinogen, DMBA, and 68% of them developed mammary tumors. Of the 39 animals that were injected with DMBA and then sulforaphane, only 26% developed tumors. Preliminary studies with rats also show promising results in preventing colon and skin cancer.

Blueberries

Blueberries deliver a potent antioxidant punch according to research from the USDA (United States Department of Agriculture). They rank among the highest in antioxidant activity compared to 40 other commercially available fruits and vegetables, according to the Jean Mayer USDA Nutrition Research Centre on Aging at Tufts University.

A laboratory testing procedure called ORAC (Oxygen Radical Absorbance

Did You Know...

Women in an Italian study who ate the fewest vegetables were 25% more likely to get breast cancer than those who ate at least five servings a day.

Capacity), recognized as the definitive measurement of antioxidant capacity, claims that blueberries are one of the top performing fruits. Early findings suggest that eating plenty of high-ORAC fruits and vegetables such as spinach and blueberries may help slow down the aging process in both mind and body. Below is a table showing you the ORAC value (antioxidant capacity) of some common fruits and vegetables.

Health Tip

Phytonutrients are more powerful when consumed with the antioxidants vitamin C, vitamin E and the mineral selenium.

Table 7-1: ORAC Value of common fruits and vegetables

Vegetables		Fruits	
Kale	1770	Prunes	5770
Spinach	1260	Raisins	2830
Brussels sprouts	980	Blueberries	2400
Alfalfa sprouts	930	Blackberries	2036
Broccoli florets	890	Strawberries	1540
Beets	840	Raspberries	1220
Red bell peppers	710	Plums	949
Onions	450	Oranges	750
Corn	400	Red grapes	739
Eggplant	390	Cherries	670

** Serving size of about 3.5 ounces (98g)

Blueberries are not only amazing antioxidants, they also appear to improve motor skills and reverse short term memory loss that comes with aging. The next time you lose your keys, grab a handful of blueberries! They also contain compounds that prevent bacteria from attaching to the bladder wall and, in practical terms that may mean a reduced risk for urinary tract infections.

Blueberries also work wonders for tired eyes, help prevent night blindness and inhibit both the initiation and promotion stages of cancer. Whether baked in a pie or sprinkled raw on your cereal (or even salad), they provide you with the same wonderful benefits. They taste great and keep you healthy - how can you go wrong?

Fast Fact

One cup of blueberries delivers as much antioxidant power as five servings of other fruits and vegetables - such as peas, carrots, apples and squash.

Grape skin polyphenols

You do your best to avoid fatty foods and alcohol because you know they're so bad for your health. Feeling virtuous, you then read a report that claims people who live in the Southwest of France, notorious for its fat ducks and geese and a high alcohol intake, are known for their longevity. How is that possible? Researchers have scratched their heads over this for years - it's known as the French Paradox.

A worldwide study by the World Health Organization showed that France has one of the lowest death rates from heart disease in the industrialized world, despite the French habits of smoking, eating fatty foods and shunning exercise. Only the Japanese, with their low-fat diet of fish and rice had a lower rate. There's a growing suspicion that the French consumption of red wine may be responsible. Could this be because of the phytonutrients found in red grapes?

In particular, scientists are turning their attention to a class of phytochemicals called "polyphenols", found abundantly in the skins and seeds of grapes. Research shows that these compounds may protect the body against chronic disease.

Grape and wine polyphenols work as antioxidants. Free radical damage to fats such as cholesterol in the bloodstream is a major precursor to heart disease. These compounds also work to control blood pressure, and reduce the occurrence of blood clots, which helps to keep the blood flowing throughout the body.

Resveratrol is one of the many polyphenols found in grapes, and is being studied for its benefits to humans. Plants suffer from environmental stress, and this is when resveratrol kicks in. Plants produce resveratrol when they are under attack by fungi, bacteria or viruses. Studies are now ongoing to see if resveratrol performs the same function in humans as well.

It now appears that it may have both antioxidant and anti-inflammatory properties. Resveratrol is unique because of its ability to battle cancer at all three steps of the cancer process - initiation, promotion and progression. It's working for you, every step of the way!

Conclusion

Phytonutrients may well be our strongest weapon against the toxins that we consume and therefore our strongest ally against body pollution. Think of these phenomenal little powerhouses as providing you with a suit of armor. They may not be essential in terms of maintaining life but they're certainly essential in maintaining health. And frankly, what's one without the other?

Begin now - today - to double your intake of fruits and vegetables! Keep it up and the results will be a dramatic increase in your protection against body pollution. It's never too late to start and never too early to begin to protect yourself against the environmental assault you face on a daily basis. Those of us inhabiting the planet today cannot afford to take our health for granted. We need to be well informed and proactive in making sure the body gets the nutrients it needs on a daily basis. This includes a rich variety of phytonutrients daily.

Take Action Today

1. *Ensure your daily diet contains a minimum of 5 servings of fruits and vegetables in a variety of colours.*

2. *For the maximum in protection from body pollution, choose fruits and vegetables with the highest ORAC value as outlined in our chart.*

3. *Supplement your daily diet with a high quality fruit and vegetable extract supplement - ideally one with additional antioxidant vitamins and minerals added.*

Table 7-2: Phytonutrient Chart

Class	Phyto-nutrient	Food Source	Focus of Current Research	Anti-oxidant
Carotenoids	Lycopene	Tomatoes, watermelon, grapefruit and guava, red peppers	Macular degeneration Cardiovascular disease, Immune function Cancer risk reduction	✓
	Lutein	Green vegetables like spinach, kale, collard greens, romaine lettuce, leeks, peas, kiwi fruit	Macular degeneration; cataracts; lung cancer	
	Zeaxanthin	Eggs, citrus, corn, spinach	Eyesight	
Flavonoids	Resveratrol	Red grapes, wine, peanuts	Atherosclerosis Cancer risk reduction	✓
	Anthocyanins	Cherries, berries, eggplant skin, red cabbage, kiwi fruit	Cataracts Cancer risk reduction	
	Quercetins	Citrus, apples, onions, parsley, green tea, red wine, cherries, broccoli, garlic, kale	Atherosclerosis Peptic Ulcer Retinopathy Hayfever High cholesterol Diabetes Asthma Cancer risk reduction Inflammation	
	Catechins	Tea, grapes, wine	Atherosclerosis Cancer risk reduction Gingivitis (periodontal disease) High cholesterol Immune function	
Phytoestrogens	Isoflavones: Genistein and Daidzein	Soybeans, and soy based products	Heart disease Cancer risk reduction High cholesterol Menopause Osteoporosis	
	Lignans	Flax or sesame seeds, whole grains and some berries	Cancer risk reduction High triglycerides High cholesterol	
Allium Compounds	Allyl Methyl Trisulfide and Diallyl Sulfide	Garlic, onions, leeks, shallots, chives	Antimicrobial Immune function Cardiovascular protection Activate liver detox enzymes Cancer risk reduction	✓

Table 7-2: Phytonutrient Chart

Class	Phyto-nutrient	Food Source	Focus of Current Research	Anti-oxidant
Gluco-sinolates	Sulforaphane	Broccoli, cauliflower, cabbage and kale	Activate liver detox enzymes Cancer risk reduction Immune function	✓
Limonoids	Limonene	Citrus peels/oils	Cancer risk reduction Activation of detox enzymes	✓

CHAPTER

The Marvelous Benefits of Fibre

Health Tip

Adding a high-fibre supplement to your diet is a convenient and effective way to increase your daily fibre intake.

For centuries, fibre was considered a throw-away. After all, it was indigestible, didn't provide nourishment and had to be useless…or so the thinking went. So apples were peeled, flour was processed, bread crusts were thrown out and everyone lived happily ever after. Well, not quite - there was trouble in paradise. A number of perplexing diseases such as diabetes, certain types of cancer, chronic digestive problems, and heart conditions increased in both incidence and severity. Something was clearly wrong. The modern world and its refined diet - a state-of-the-art diet in the richest parts of the world - based on meat and processed food wasn't working. Fibre, it turns out, was one of the major missing elements.

While a few voices in the wilderness were proclaiming the importance of fibre, it wasn't until 1971 that its true value was confirmed unequivocally. British physician Dennis Burkett found a surprisingly low incidence of certain diseases such as hernias, hemorrhoids, diabetes, diverticulitis (small pouches in the large intestine), heart disease and bowel disease among the people he worked with in rural Africa. He attributed this to native diets rich in whole grains, seeds, roots, vegetables and nuts and blamed the modern world's high incidence of these disorders on a lack of dietary fibre. Burkett's 'Bran Hypothesis' swept around the world and was enthusiastically adopted. Since that time, the link between good health and dietary fibre has been reconfirmed over and over again.

Fibre is finally recognized for the essential health tool it truly is. Let me begin by defining it - fibre is an indigestible complex carbohydrate found only in plant food such as grains, vegetables and fruit. It actually forms the skeletal basis of plants and without it, no plant or tree would stand upright.

Did You Know...

Following the 5 A Day recommendation of fruits and vegetables not only increases your phytonutrients but your fibre as well.

Some nutritionists believe that virtually every meal we eat should contain some fibre. It turns out that the meat that was once thought to be so essential to life actually isn't and the fibre that was once thought to be so unimportant actually is. Now that's true progress!

Fast Fact

The National Cancer Institute recommends adults consume between 25 and 35 grams of dietary fibre a day.

Fortunately, the role of fibre in our diet is becoming much more apparent. Fibre acts as natures scrub brush for our intestine. With our fast-paced lifestyles, polluted environment and poor-quality diet, we often accumulate waste matter in the lining of the intestinal tract which prevents the absorption of nutrients and causes toxic overload. The buildup of toxins in the intestines is one of the end results of body pollution and can lead to a multitude of problems including poor nutritional status, low energy levels and disease. Thankfully, we have fibre to 'scrub' this waste away, encourage regular bowel movements and maintain a healthy intestine.

Another benefit of fibre is that it provides no calories. Since we lack the enzymes to break it down, it's not absorbed and is simply passed through the digestive system.

Soluble vs. Insoluble Fibre

There are two different kinds of fibre - water soluble and water insoluble - and we need both. Each functions differently in the body providing unique health benefits. Most foods contain both types of fibre in varying ratios so don't worry about what kind you're getting, just make sure you get lots of it! You really can't go wrong here.

Soluble Fibre	Insoluble Fibre
• May lower blood cholesterol and help control blood sugar. • Plays a role in cancer prevention and heart health. Sources include: Oat products (oatmeal, oatbran), legumes (dried beans, peas and lentils) and pectin-rich fruits (apples, strawberries and citrus fruits).	• Helps promote bowel regularity. • Prevent and control bowel problems and certain cancers. • Acts as a natural cleanser, moving solid waste through your intestines. Sources include: Wheat bran, whole-grain foods, beans and the skin, stems leaves and seeds of vegetables and fruit.

Health Benefits of Fibre

Heart Disease

Soluble fibre helps keep your heart healthy and participants of the Smart Heart Challenge in the U.S. proved it. During the 30-day challenge, participants volunteered to eat a bowl of oatmeal daily to prove to themselves that a simple lifestyle change could reduce cholesterol levels. The results were dramatic. After 30 days, 70% lowered their cholesterol.

The American Heart Association also reports that soluble fibre binds with serum cholesterol and helps prevent it from being absorbed into the bloodstream. Reducing serum cholesterol is one of the most effective defenses against heart disease. In clinical studies at the University of Kentucky, adding just 3 1/2 ounces of oat bran to the daily diet reduced cholesterol by an average of 13% over a period of just 10 days.

So your grandmother was on the right track - eating your oatmeal is a really good idea. In fact, the FDA awarded the first-ever food specific health claim to oat products because of their heart-healthy benefits. This was because three grams of soluble fibre from oatmeal daily, in a diet low in saturated fat and cholesterol, may reduce the risk of heart disease.

Diabetes

It seems soluble fibre may also play a role in preventing and controlling diabetes. Diabetics who add more high-fibre fruit, vegetables and grains can improve their blood sugar levels and may reduce their need for medicine, researchers report in the *New England Journal of Medicine*.

The binding action of soluble fibre helps slow the entry of glucose into the bloodstream. Recent studies by the American Diabetes Association prove that high-fibre diets consistently improve glucose tolerance and lower insulin needs. Here's how it works - soluble fibre absorbs many different toxic materials from the intestinal tract and it also helps regulate the absorption rate of nutrients, especially sugar, spreading it over a longer period of time. The result is a slower rise in blood-sugar level and a less rapid subsequent drop which is very important to diabetics.

Cancer

Insoluble fibre, also known as roughage, helps promote bowel regularity and prevents and controls bowel problems and certain cancers. It acts as a natural laxative,

Did You Know...

Oat beta glucan is thought to be the active ingredient responsible for the heart healthy properties of oat fibre.

moving solid waste through the intestines. The fibre passes through the digestive system intact while the nutrients it carries get absorbed into the body.

The National Cancer Institute links insoluble dietary fibre to a reduced risk of colorectal cancer. In fact, some scientists estimate that by the turn of the century, more than 20,000 cases of large bowel cancer could be prevented every year simply by adding more fibre to the diet.

Health Tip

High-fibre snacks between meals will help you feel full until your next meal so you avoid snacking on junk foods.

Fast Fact

Colon cancer is the third most common cancer among men and women in the U.S. Over 93,000 people are diagnosed each year - 43,400 cases in men and 50,400 cases in women.

The current theory for these anti-cancer causing effects is that fibre either dilutes cancer-causing chemicals (from body pollution) in the colon, or that it ushers the chemicals out before they can have prolonged contact with the colon wall. Both insoluble and soluble fibre helps to decrease cancer-causing effects. Soluble fibre helps to attract these chemicals to it and insoluble fibre aids in accelerating the movement of these chemicals out of the colon.

Summary of Fibre Benefits:

Fights Body Pollution
✓ Fibre is a miracle worker behind the scenes, cleansing toxins and waste material out the body before toxic buildup can occur.

Combats Constipation
✓ The most undisputed advantage of insoluble fibre is its ability to soften and expand stool volume, speeding up fecal transit and elimination.

Improves Diabetic Control
✓ Soluble fibre from legumes, barley, oats, some fruit and vegetables can help regulate blood-sugar control.

Heart Health
✓ Excess blood fats such as cholesterol may be reduced by soluble fibres such as pectin, bean and oat gums, and the types in legumes (lentils, chickpeas, navy, pinto or kidney beans).

Possible protection against cancer

✓ Fibre may dilute cancer-causing chemicals in the colon, or usher the chemicals out before they can have prolonged contact with the colon wall.

Daily Recommendations for Fibre

Are you getting enough? Probably not. Most adults aren't. In spite of all of the health-promoting qualities of fibre, the average adult is still only consuming between 10-15g each day - far short of the recommended 25-35g per day.

As discussed in Chapter 3, food processing strips much of our food of essential nutrients and fibre by separating the bran and germ (fibre), leaving only the endosperm and huge volumes of fine white flour.

Remember the entrepreneurial flour millers who developed a lucrative market for these "by-products" of the milling process. The bran and germ were being made into highly nutritious animal feed for chickens and cattle. The millers refused to return the bran and germ to the flour and chose instead to "enrich" certain products. But we all know what that means - the fiber content is not replaced.

Fast Fact

A chicken sandwich made with white bread contains 1.5 grams of dietary fibre. The same chicken sandwich made on whole wheat bread has 5 grams of fibre.

The lack of fibre in most diets concerns me since the benefits are so wide-reaching. Fibre is vital for people of all ages, including children. Children who eat a wide variety of food rich in fibre are likely to continue eating these foods in later years. Children over the age of 5 should gradually add more fibre to their diet.

The rule of thumb used to calculate the amount of fibre children need each day is this - the child's "age plus five". For example, an 8 year old child would need 13 grams of fiber each day (8 + 5 = 13). After 18, the adult recommendation for fibre would apply.

Let me remind you that if you or your children are not used to high-fibre foods, you need to gradually increase your intake to avoid bloating and cramps. Focus

Did You Know...

Women who eat cereal frequently weigh about 8 pounds less on average that those who don't. Men who eat cereal frequently weigh about 6 pounds less on average than men who eat cereal less often.

on a higher-fibre breakfast for the first week and then make another change the following week, to give your digestive system a chance to adjust.

Okay, you're convinced that getting the right amount of fibre is essential to your health. Now what? I want to reassure you that changing your habits is not as daunting as it may appear. Gradual changes soon begin to add up and if you persevere, you'll soon benefit from the wonderful bonus of reclaiming your health and energy.

Health Tip

Boost the fibre of your salads by adding raisins, nuts, shredded carrots, apple slices or sun-flower seeds.

Here are a few simple tips to increase your fibre intake:

1. Start your day with a high-fibre cereal. Have fun combining a variety of cereals. Add 1-2 Tbsp. of psyllium, oat bran or wheat germ to your favourite.

2. Choose whole-grain breads, buns, pitas, bagels, crackers, etc. (e.g. whole wheat, oatbran, pumpernickel, multi-grain).

3. Enjoy legumes (chickpeas, beans, etc.) at least once or twice a week. Toss legumes into your soups, salads, pasta sauces. Try bean spreads and dips.

4. Enjoy at least one or two servings of fruit or vegetables at every meal.

5. Enrich your diet with a high-fibre food supplement.

Today's diet consists primarily of refined, processed and convenience foods -- because of this, very few people meet the necessary fibre requirements. With a few simple changes, you'll find increasing your fibre intake is quite easy.

To help guide your decisions, here's a chart showing the fibre content of some common foods: (next page)

Table 8-1: Amount of fibre found in certain foods.

Food	Serving size	Total fibre (grams)	Soluble fibre (grams)	Insoluble fibre (grams)
English muffin	1	2.0	0.5	1.5
Whole Wheat Pita	1 large (6.5 in)	4.74	2.09	2.65
Spaghetti, cooked	1 cup	2.0	0.5	1.5
Whole-wheat bread	1 slice	2.5	0.5	2.0
White rice, cooked	1/2 cup	0.5	0	0.5
Brown rice, cooked	1/2 cup	1.75	0.20	1.56
Bran flake cereal	3/4 cup	5.5	0.5	5.0
Corn flake cereal	1 cup	1.0	0	1.0
Oatmeal, cooked	3/4 cup	3.0	1.0	2.0
Banana	1 medium	2.0	0.5	1.5
Apple, with skin	1 medium	3.0	0.5	2.5
Orange	1 medium	2.0	0.5	1.5
Pear, with skin	1 medium	4.5	0.5	4.0
Strawberries	1/2 cup	1.0	0	1.0
Broccoli	1/2 cup	2.0	0	2.0
Corn	1/2 cup	1.5	0	1.5
Potato, baked with skin	1 medium	4.0	1.0	3.0
Spinach	1/2 cup	2.0	0.5	1.5
Kidney beans	1/2 cup	4.5	1.0	3.5
Chickpeas	1/2 cup	6.32	1.94	4.30
Popcorn	1 cup	1.0	0	1.0
Peanut butter, chunky	2 tablespoons	1.5	0	1.5

Health Tip

When increasing your fibre intake, increase you consumption of water as well. Extra water will help the fibre to remove more toxins from the body.

Conclusion

By now, you have a clear vision of the many ingredients that make up vibrant health. Everything you've read so far in this book overlaps and adds up to great health. Increasing fruits and vegetables for example will not only raise your daily level of vitamins and minerals but also your phytonutrient intake and fibre. A return to whole, natural food is the answer, not only to increase fibre intake but to provide your body with the many nutrients needed to combat body pollution.

Take Action Today

1. *Start adding more fibre-rich food to your diet to help fight body pollution and cleanse your digestive system.*

2. *Eat a wide variety of fibre foods to ensure you're getting the health benefits of both soluble and insoluble fibre.*

3. *Add a high-fibre supplement to your diet to make sure you're reaching the recommended daily intake of 25-35 grams.*

CHAPTER

Obesity: A Global Epidemic

If you were taught as a child, to clean off your plate, you're not alone. Almost all of us feel a little guilty about 'wasting' good food and not finishing off a serving. There's no doubt that it's wasteful to throw perfectly good food out. It would be very nice if somehow it could be mailed to someone who really needed it. But that can't be done and the fact is, for the first time in history, there are more of us in this world suffering the ill effects of overeating than there are people starving. So even if we could mail our leftovers, we'd quickly run out of people to mail them to. Return to sender might apply, I'm afraid!

Fast Fact

The typical dinner plate at a restaurant has grown to an average diameter of 12 inches compared with the standard home dinner plate which is nine inches.

The World Health Organization gives us some shocking statistics - they estimate that 300 million people worldwide are obese and 750 million more are overweight. With the rapid rise in obesity, the standards of what constitutes an abnormal level of body fat may have to be redefined. It seems that overweight is the new norm.

But no amount of adjusted standards can turn eating too much into a healthy activity. Eating more food than your body can use is worse than wasteful, it's actu-

Did You Know...

ally harmful. At least what we throw out isn't hurting anyone. Next time you're at a fancy restaurant and feel that you've eaten all that you want or need, remind yourself that it's better to stop there than to overburden your body. Keep in mind that overeating, even if it's good food, can be another form of body pollution. If you consistently overeat, you're increasing your body's storage space in the form of excess fat.

There's a difference between being overweight and being obese. Overweight simply means weighing too much. While some people might be overweight due to large bone structures or athletic muscle mass the majority of the population is simply carrying around too much fat. Being obese is taking this even one step further and having an abnormally high proportion of body fat.

Health experts use a scientific measurement called the Body Mass Index (BMI) to figure out whether or not you have a healthy weight. To make it easy for you to measure, here's a chart that will show you your BMI in four easy steps:

1. Find your height in one of the first two columns
2. Slide your finger across to find your weight in pounds
3. Slide finger up to find your BMI number (19-35)
4. Check along top line to see where your BMI falls (underweight, ideal, overweight or obese)

Table 9-1 Body Mass Index Finder

Underweight (<18.5)		Ideal(19-24)						Overweight (25-29)					Obese(>30)					
Height	**in inches**	**19**	**20**	**21**	**22**	**23**	**24**	**25**	**26**	**27**	**28**	**29**	**30**	**31**	**32**	**33**	**34**	**35**
4'10"	58"	91	96	100	105	110	115	119	124	129	134	138	143	148	153	158	162	167
4'11"	59"	94	99	104	109	114	119	124	128	133	138	143	148	153	158	163	168	173
5'0"	60"	97	102	107	112	118	123	128	133	138	143	148	153	158	163	168	174	179
5'1"	61"	100	106	111	116	122	127	132	137	143	148	153	158	164	169	174	180	185
5'2"	62"	104	109	115	120	126	131	136	142	147	153	158	163	169	175	180	186	191
5'3"	63"	107	113	118	124	130	135	141	146	152	158	164	169	175	180	186	191	197
5'4"	64"	110	116	122	128	134	140	145	151	157	163	169	174	180	186	192	197	204
5'5"	65"	114	120	126	132	138	144	150	156	162	168	174	180	186	192	198	204	210	216
5'6"	66"	118	124	130	136	142	148	155	161	167	173	179	186	192	198	204	210	216
5'7"	67"	121	127	134	140	146	153	159	166	172	178	185	191	198	204	211	217	223
5'8"	68"	125	131	138	144	151	158	164	171	177	184	190	197	203	210	216	223	230
5'9"	69"	128	135	142	149	155	162	169	176	182	189	196	203	209	216	223	230	236
5'10"	70"	132	139	146	153	160	167	174	181	188	195	202	209	216	222	229	236	242
5'11"	71"	136	143	150	157	165	172	179	186	193	200	208	215	222	229	236	243	250
6'0"	72"	140	147	154	162	169	177	184	191	199	206	213	221	228	236	242	250	258
6'1"	73"	144	151	159	166	174	182	189	197	204	212	219	227	235	242	250	257	265
6'2"	74"	148	155	163	171	179	186	194	202	210	218	225	233	241	249	256	264	272
6'3"	75"	152	160	168	176	184	192	200	208	216	224	232	240	248	256	264	272	279
6'4"	76"	156	164	172	180	189	197	205	213	221	230	238	246	254	263	271	279	287

Prevalence of Obesity (Adults)

It took almost 30 years for the negative health effects of the overindulgent western lifestyle to show up but today's obesity epidemic is evidence few can miss. Sadly, it's quickly being exported with every fast-food restaurant that sprouts up in countries around the world. Others have adopted North America's seemingly 'trendy' bad habits and the health effects are showing up almost instantaneously.

Fast-food restaurants made serious inroads in China in the 1990's, and the number of people eating a high-fat diet soon rose from 23% to 87%. The number of overweight people increased from 9% to 15%. Still a far cry from the U.S. where 61% of adults are considered overweight. Obesity has increased by up to 40% in some European countries and in Japan, one in three males is overweight. Part of this alarming increase in Japan can be attributed to fast-food chains now seen everywhere, offering among other things, a Japanese favourite - pizza topped with mayonnaise. The people suffering the most from obesity can be found in the South Pacific which has exchanged a physically active culture for what may be the world's highest rates of obesity. This seems like a losing exchange to me.

Obesity in Children

There are many ways that children can be harmed, both intentionally and unintentionally, but one of the worst things we can do to our children is to teach them bad eating habits. By doing this, we're handing our children bad health on a platter. Teaching them to eat poorly will affect every aspect of their lives - their appearance along with their emotional and physical health. These bad habits may well last a lifetime. At least half of obese children over age six and 70-80% of obese adolescents become obese adults.

When we indulge children by giving them junk food or neglect to teach them the principles of good nutrition from the very beginning, it can have serious repercussions. The International Obesity Task Force estimates that 22 million of the world's children are overweight or obese. In the U. S., 27% of 10 year olds are overweight or obese, the third-highest percentage in the world behind Malta (33%) and Italy (29%). A recent survey done in Canada showed that over half of Canadian children are overweight at some point in their childhood years.

Even in some areas of Africa, there are more children who are overweight than starving. Poor countries are also at risk for obesity since junk food that provides calories without providing nutrition is usually inexpensive and therefore acces-

Health Tip

White meats generally contain less fat then dark meats. Turkey is one of the lowest fat meats and makes a great low-fat sandwich.

Did You Know...

sible to almost everyone. It's the nutrient-rich food that's harder to come by. While we tend to be indulgent about a child putting on a few extra pounds, it's important to be vigilant about your children's weight.

It's more than just a cosmetic issue - being overweight or obese is a risk factor for several major diseases and chronic health problems. Children are our future and we owe it to them to teach them healthy habits that will last a lifetime. Otherwise, they could be in for serious health problems as you'll see in the next section.

General Health Risks of Being Overweight or Obese

The World Health Organization has predicted that obesity could soon have as great an impact on health as smoking. Obesity is a risk factor for four of the 10 leading causes of death in the world: heart disease, diabetes, stroke and cancer. In the U.S., obesity accounts for more than 300,000 premature deaths each year and costs the health care system more than $61 billion annually! Let's have a look at a few of the negative health implications obesity is related to.

Heart Disease

The risk of heart failure doubles in obese people and is one-third higher in overweight people, according to the *New England Journal of Medicine*. In addition to this, the life span for overweight people is shorter - on average, they develop heart disease seven years earlier than those of normal weight.

Cancer

As we age, the pounds tend to keep creeping up. Is this a cause for concern or should we accept it as a natural consequence of aging?

It's your choice - I would just urge you to make it an informed one. Before you answer this question, consider that as small a weight gain as half a pound per year or five pounds per decade can increase your risk of cancer.

We know that our risk of heart disease and diabetes rises right along with the scales, but very few people are aware that the cancer risk also increases. One-quarter to one-third of cancer cases around the world are linked to being overweight and physically inactive.

Diabetes

As rates of obesity rise, so does the incidence of diabetes. Type 2 diabetes used to be called adult onset diabetes because it was so rare in children. No longer! Now children as young as 10 years old have been diagnosed with the disease and the number of children and adolescents with the condition (most diagnosed in their early teens) has skyrocketed within the last 20 years. No wonder the journal Diabetes Care calls it an 'emerging epidemic'. In the U.S., experts estimate that 10-20 percent of all cases of childhood and adolescent diabetes are now Type 2, compared with only 2 to 3 percent a few years ago.

As for a link to obesity, nearly 80 percent of patients with type 2 diabetes are obese. This emerging epidemic could cause untold hardships and cost millions. Diabetes doesn't tend to strike the same fear in our hearts as cancer does, maybe because it can be controlled. Or maybe because people just aren't aware of the implications which can include amputation, blindness, kidney failure and much more. This is an illness that truly takes away the quality of life and often, it's easily preventable.

Reasons for Obesity

Slow metabolism? Genetic legacy? These are very rarely causes of obesity and overweight.

Our changing eating habits are a major contributing factor in the battle of the bulge. Most of us are time-starved and often opt for fast food which isn't always as nutritious as a home-cooked meal. And restaurant portion sizes are also increasing.

Our sedentary lifestyles are also part of the obesity equation. While a super-active person can get away with consuming too many calories from time to time, someone whose work requires them to sit most of the day will find that any excess calories end up being stored as fat if exercise isn't part of their regular routine.

The environment we're surrounded by today encourages us to overeat and gain weight. All of the above factors play a role in the global obesity epidemic as we'll soon see.

Changing Diet Patterns

Our love affair with fast and processed food is growing almost as quickly as our

Did You Know...

Fat cells can keep cancer causing chemicals trapped in the body, which can lead to the development of the disease.

waistlines and with good reason. In the 1950's, a typical fast-food meal was approximately 590 calories. Today it averages 1550 calories which is almost a full day's requirement with very few nutrients such as vitamins, minerals and fibre.

While the government recommends no more than 3 to 6 ounces of meat daily, the smallest steak available at the average restaurant is 8 ounces and 24 ounce steaks and 32 ounce drinks are becoming the new norm. Even the muffins at coffee shops are super-sized. Maybe that's because it doesn't cost vendors much to increase portion size and allows them to up the price. Do I smell the profit factor here?

There is certainly profit to be had. In 1970, Americans spent about $6 billion on fast food and in the year 2000 that amount went up to $110 billion. Americans now spend more money on fast food than on higher education, personal computers, or new cars. This isn't just an American thing; in the 1980's as many as five new fast food restaurants opened everyday - four of these were outside of the U.S. Seems our love of fast food is international.

Concerned about the battle of the bulge, some people are wisely avoiding saturated fat but unwisely substituting food with a high-sugar content. That low-fat muffin could well be loaded with sugar! Low fat, does not always mean low calorie - often when manufacturers reduce fat, they load up on sugars to improve the taste and the caloric content of the two products ends up very similar.

Let's look into this a little further as I think it's an important point. Per gram, fat contains more calories than sugar - but in the end it's the total number of calories that count.

Table 9-2: Caloric content of Macronutrients

Macronutrient	Calories per Gram
Fat	9 cal/g
Protein	4 cal/g
Carbohydrate	4 cal/g
Alcohol	7 cal/g

In practical terms, what does this mean? The can of cola, and the glass of wine, although they contain no fat, are actually the same in calories as the sliver of cheesecake we all try to avoid.

While most high-fat foods are high in calories, don't be mislead by high-sugar foods as these can pack a powerful calorie punch too!

A calorie is a calorie is a calorie, regardless of the source, and if you consistently eat more than you need, your body converts that calorie to fat and stores it in some convenient warehouse - like your hips or your waistline! Carbonated soft drinks are the greatest offenders and are the single biggest source of refined sugars in modern diets. The average teenager gets 7 teaspoons of sugar a day from soft drink consumption - that's 2555 teaspoons of sugar a year or 41,200 calories a year from drinks with absolutely no nutritional value.

Governments around the world have jumped on the low-fat bandwagon and their campaign to reduce saturated fat in daily diets has had an effect. But not the effect they aimed for. Since the campaign started in North America, calorie intake is up by 400 per day - a major contribution to obesity. People are apparently substituting sugar for fat. This reinforces my point that you have to watch not only what you eat but also how much you eat.

Sedentary Lifestyle

An active, healthy person who is not overweight can over-indulge from time to time without paying too high a price for it. That person becomes harder and harder to find in a society that encourages us to stay at home and watch television along with its food-inspiring ads.

Fast Fact

60 - 85 percent of the global population is not physically active.

Our bodies end up being in a constant battle with our evolutionary ancestors who lead very active lifestyles and had to hunt for their food. Storing extra calories as fat was an evolutionary advantage for our Paleolithic ancestors since the fat helped them survive the inevitable famines. We, on the other hand, sit at computers all day and in front of the television at night. Hardly an active lifestyle.

How to Avoid the Battle of the Bulge

We all know that being overweight is unhealthy but what can we do about it? When reading about dieting, you're bound to get confused about what works and what's healthy. There are low-fat diets competing with low-carbohydrate diets for your 'diet' dollar - one of them must be wrong but which one? It's difficult sorting through all the information.

Fast Fact

Americans spend $33 billion annually on weight-loss products and services.

Health Tip

To maximize your body's fat burning systems, eat smaller meals every three to four hours.

A Healthy Diet

Concerned about the confusion in the marketplace, the U.S. Department of Agriculture sponsored the Great Nutrition Debate in 2000 bringing together famous diet doctors like Robert Atkins (low carbohydrate, high protein) and Dean Ornish (low fat, plant-based) to advocate their differing approaches to weight loss. To further help consumers find their way through the maze, the USDA studied the effectiveness of varying weight-loss approaches. Initial findings concluded that regardless of approach, limiting total daily calorie consumption was the most important factor in successful weight loss.

Right! Now what? Well, a calorie is a unit of energy that the body obtains from food. Here's the simple truth. If you eat more calories than you burn, you'll gain weight. Even if those calories come from a nutrient dense organic piece of freshly picked fruit. I know - it just doesn't seem fair, does it, but understanding that solid principle is critical to managing your weight. If you eat fewer calories than you burn, you'll lose weight.   Simple, right?

One pound of body fat is approximately equal to 3500 calories. While this seems like a lot, a reduction of 500 calories a day, for 7 days will result in a loss of one pound per week. This may seem minimal at first, but consider that in just 6 months, you will have lost nearly 25 pounds - a very significant amount!

Now all you need to know is how many calories you need on a daily basis and how many calories your favourite foods contain in order to make wiser choices consistently.

Use this simple example as a guideline to calculate how many calories you need.

1. Start with your current weight.
2. If you're female multiply this by 11, if you're male multiply it by 12.

This gives you your base calorie requirement to perform basic body functions like breathing. As we age, our metabolism slows down because we lose lean muscle mass which is calorie-burning tissue. To factor in your age to this equation...

3. Subtract 2% for every decade over 20 you are from your base calorie requirement to get your age adjusted calorie requirement.

Because most of us do more everyday than just perform regular body functions...

4. Add an additional 10% to the age adjusted calorie requirement to factor in daily activities.

This number is the approximate amount of calories needed to maintain the weight you are at right now.

Did You Know...

You need to eat 3,500 calories in order to gain one pound or burn that same amount in order to lose one pound.

A 130 pound woman for example, needs <u>1430</u> (11 x 130) calories a day to perform basic bodily functions

If this woman was 40 years old, she would subtract 4% (2 decades above 20) from 1430, her base calorie requirement.

4% of 1430 = 57
1430 - 57 = <u>1373</u> calories

1373 is the age adjusted calorie requirement to perform basic bodily functions.

10% of 1373 is 137.
1373 +137 = 1510

<u>1510</u> is the amount of calories needed for a 40 year old, 130 pound woman who is not regularly physically active to maintain her current weight.

Now that we've learned a little bit about calorie requirements, its worth a final reminder that no matter what the source of your extra calories - protein, carbo-hydrates or fat - if you eat more than your body can use, they'll be stored as fat and you'll gain weight. Restricting your calories is a good idea but, in this world of body pollution, you can't afford to restrict your nutrients. Make sure what you do eat is nutrient-rich.

In an effort to help the public make healthy food choices, five leading health organizations in the U.S. have jointly endorsed a healthy eating plan - this can serve as an example for us all.

Health Tip

When on a weight management program, never skip meals or allotted snacks - this often leads to overeating later in the evening.

The American Cancer Society, the American Dietetic Association, the American Academy of Pediatrics, the National Institutes of Health and the American Heart Association recommend a diet based on balance of the right amounts of fats, starches, fibre, fruits, vegetables, protein and so on. Funny, this is exactly what we've talked about all along! It just makes sense.

Take another look at our Lifestyle Pyramid to refresh your memory on the basics of a good diet. In Chapter Three, I talked about the changing diet and what nutrients you need to fight body pollution. By following the Lifestyle Pyramid, you won't need to calculate what percentage of carbohydrates you've eaten that day, you just need to choose foods that fall at the bottom of the pyramid more frequently and limit those at the top. Getting all the nutrients you need doesn't have to be complicated, it will just naturally fall into place. Don't be too hard on yourself if you slip now and again. It works just the same as a financial investment - it's what you do over the long term that counts.

While the concept of weight loss seems fairly easy, it can be a challenge for many of us. Thankfully, there is help available.

Meal Replacements

Meal replacements can be a fat-fighting tool. Let's say an average meal for you contains 500 calories and you have a meal replacement substitute of 250 calories - you've just cut your calories for that meal in half. Doing this twice on a daily basis means that you could reduce your caloric intake by 500 calories per day. Recall that 3500 calories is approximately equal to one pound. When used in conjunction with healthy foods, high-quality meal replacements are an excellent way to reduce your caloric intake while still getting adequate nutrients. An example of this might be a well-balanced nutritious meal replacement for breakfast and lunch, two healthy snacks and then a sensible meal for dinner.

For those of us who are time-strapped but still want to eat well, fast food is not your only option. A meal replacement makes a lot of sense.

You'll want a replacement that's balanced in protein, fat and carbohydrate, rich in vitamins and minerals and in a nutrient-dense format that's not inclined to promote significant body fat storage. On average, each serving should provide approximately 250 calories.

Fibre

Fibre is another weight and hunger control tool. It removes unwanted fats and toxins from the body and, since it absorbs more than its weight in water, gives you a feeling of being full. A high-fibre snack can be a great in-between meal choice. Certainly beats a chocolate bar!

Exercise

Exercise also plays a role in weight loss by jumpstarting your metabolism and we'll talk about it in more detail in another chapter. In fact, if you exercise early in the day, you'll give your metabolism a boost.

Revving up your metabolism means that you burn up more calories - a truly painless way of losing weight. There are certain herbs that also stimulate your metabolism and assist in weight loss.

Citrus Aurantium

Citrus Aurantium, sometimes known as bitter orange extract was used in traditional Chinese medicine for thousands of years to treat chest congestion and indigestion, stimulate gastrointestinal functions and improve circulation and liver function.

Exciting research has uncovered new properties of this versatile herb. It assists in weight loss in three ways by burning fat, increasing physical performance and building lean muscle mass. All of these, of course, help increase your metabolic rate.

Untll recently, ma huang (the herb that ephedra is derived from) was the most effective herbal metabolic enhancer. But there have been serious problems with ma huang. The U.S. FDA claims it can sometimes cause negative amphetamine-like side effects such as elevated blood pressure, muscle disturbances, insomnia, dry mouth, heart palpitations and nervousness. Some of the compounds in ma huang are fat soluble and can cross the blood brain barrier - this is what causes irregularities in the central nervous system along with cardiovascular side effects. These are considered so serious that ephedra is now banned in many countries, including Canada.

Citrus Aurantium has the same weight-loss enhancing properties of ma huang without the dangerous side effects. The active compounds it contains are much less fat soluble and don't readily cross the blood brain barrier. The amount of this herb needed to jump start your metabolism is too low to cause an increase in either heart rate or blood pressure. So this herb is a much preferable alternative.

Fast Fact

A decade ago, movie seats were 18 inches wide - today the industry standard has been raised to 22 inches.

Phaseolamine Vulgaris (White Kidney Bean Extract)

As I've mentioned, the 'low fat' era actually caused an increase in calories - mainly in the form of starchy carbohydrates. Your body can't absorb starch directly, it needs an enzyme called amylase to break starches down into simple sugars which are then absorbed and either used for energy or stored as body fat.

White kidney bean extract has the unique ability to block amylase. Think about it. If the excess starch that you've just indulged in is interrupted on its way to sugar conversion, it won't be absorbed and won't add to your calorie count. You're off the hook! Clinical trials have shown that the consumption of white kidney bean extract can be part of a successful weight-loss program. It also reduces the dramatic spike in blood sugar levels after eating simple starches. Patients who took white kidney bean extract experienced a return to normal blood glucose levels 20 minutes earlier. Pretty impressive!

Conclusion

The basic foundation of weight control is to remember that if you consistently take in more calories than your body can burn, you'll gain weight. Excess calories, no matter what form they're in, can end up being stored in your body and become a form of body pollution.

Gaining excess weight has serious implications for your health and emotional well being. The diseases I've talked about so far - diabetes, heart conditions, cancer - are just the tip of the iceberg. it will impact every aspect of your health.

Fortunately, there are ways to help you reach or maintain a healthy weight. By doing this, not only will you feel great, but you will take a giant step towards disease prevention and optimal health.

Take Action Today

1. *Think of excess calories as a form of body pollution - consume only as many calories as you need to maintain your present weight or less to lose weight.*

2. *Follow the Lifestyle Pyramid in Chapter 3 and you will be assured a nutrient-rich, balanced diet that focuses on quality not quantity.*

3. *Use meal replacements and botanical supplements to help you lose weight faster.*

CHAPTER

Staying Young At Any Age

Health Tip

If you are physically fit, eat a healthy, balanced diet and take nutritional supplements, you can measure out to be 10 to 20 years younger biologically than your chronological age.

Getting older doesn't have to be a drag. In fact, it can be the best and most productive time of your life as long as you're healthy - that's the catch. Staying healthy as you age means you have to work a little harder at it. You need to be vigilant and well-informed about health issues. You just don't have the margin for error you had when you were younger and could get away with late nights, skipped meals, junk food and so on. Getting older is catch-up time and any bad habits you may have had in your youth begin to make themselves known. Still, it's never too late to turn things around and before long, you'll begin to reap the benefits of taking care of your health. You may find you're more fit and healthy in your fifties than you were at the age of 20. Many people do.

Equipped with a healthy body and the wisdom you've accumulated over a lifetime, you now can look forward to a long and productive life.

It's a nice time to be alive since the life span has been dramatically expanded in the last century. The life expectancy of a male child born in 1900 was only 46; yet a male child born today can expect to live more than 72 years and a female about 79 years.

Fast Fact

The average person's life span during the Roman Empire was twenty-eight years.

Did You Know...

A fifty-year-old woman's risk of dying from a hip fracture is equal to her risk of dying from breast cancer.

Unfortunately, our quality of life hasn't kept pace with the progress on longevity. Far too many people are living medically extended lives that are compromised by chronic pain, immobilization, mental deterioration and prescription drug dependency.

Let's zero in on Frank and Martha, a reasonably typical couple. Frank, in his early sixties, has been on anti-anxiety drugs for years. Now it turns out he has high blood pressure so he's taking something for that as well. The blood pressure pills have reduced his libido and as a result he's no longer interested in sex. That suits his wife, Martha, just fine. She's got health struggles of her own that take most of her attention. She's been recently diagnosed with type 2 diabetes and also suffers from osteoarthritis.

She needs a hip replacement but her surgeon refuses to operate until she quits smoking and loses twenty-five pounds. Martha and Frank have two children and three grandchildren but family gatherings just aren't much fun anymore. They don't seem to have the energy to enjoy their children the way they used to and trying to cook for a large group is simply too much work. Some days, just getting out of bed is a struggle.

Martha and Frank are a fictional couple. Unfortunately, they represent a huge segment of the population and are one reason health-care systems all over the world will soon feel an enormous strain. If we drop in on Martha and Frank in another decade, when they're in their seventies, how do you think they'll be managing? I suspect their health problems will continue to grow unless they both take drastic action. Personally, this is not how I want to spend my 'golden' years. Fortunately, I have a lot of options and choice as to how healthy I'll be - and so do you.

Fast Fact

The over-50 demographic accounts for 74% of all prescription drug purchases.

When you're young, you have some slack. You can get away with little sleep, poor diet and other abuses from time to time. While we may be more resilient in our youth, it is important to remember that what you do when you're young can have an impact on how you age. At any age, you simply can't take your health for granted. The price of ignorance is poor health.

In order to stay healthy, let's learn more about what causes aging.

What Causes Aging?

There are two main theories currently in vogue. One is that the aging process results from genetically programmed changes. This is based on the premise that every cell in your body has an "expiry date" or preset life span. If this holds true, then even if we lived in a perfectly pristine "bubble-like" environment, we would still have a predisposed lifespan. The question is, how long would that lifespan be? Under perfect conditions, how long could humans actually live? Many researchers think we could live well past 120 years under the right conditions.

The second theory is that aging occurs because of an accumulation of errors in cell functioning (damage to the DNA of the cell) that are caused by external factors. Smoking, poor diets, excessive alcohol consumption, drug use, exposure to environmental and occupational pollutants or what we collectively call body pollution, all contribute to the premature aging of a population that could otherwise live a longer and healthier life. So just living in today's toxic world can make you age more quickly than you need to.

The effects of body pollution on aging have not yet been fully acknowledged by researchers even though the available data certainly verifies the damage. Part of the problem is that pollutants are increasing so rapidly that scientists are scrambling to keep up with the research.

As we've already learned, body pollution causes an excess of free radicals. These free radicals eventually cause DNA damage which can lead to premature aging and chronic illness. This premise gained credibility with the scientific community after an ingenious experiment comparing fruit flies with and without antioxidant protection. The flies that were protected from free radicals lived up to 20% longer and remained physically active far longer into old age. This research confirms the theory that body pollution and the production of excess free radicals are a major cause of premature aging and degenerative conditions.

Health Tip

Taking vitamin E with a small amount of fat increases its antioxidant protection dramatically.

Fast Fact

Antioxidants have been correlated with life span in at least 20 species.

Did You Know...

The Japanese language has no word for 'hot flash'? Menopausal symptoms are much less frequent in Asian women and it's thought that one reason is because of their high intake of soy foods.

What Happens as We Get Older?

Let me assure you, aging doesn't have to be dismal. In fact, getting older (and wiser) can be a wonderful time in one's life. Although even healthy, natural aging involves the steady decline of organ functioning and of body systems, it's remarkable how much control we can have over this. If we take good care of our bodies, we might not even notice that we're getting older. If we don't notice, neither will anyone else!

Hormone Changes

While scientists can't agree on exactly what causes aging, there is consensus that the gradual decline of the body's hormone systems occurs in the aging process.

Quite simply, hormone production, which helps regulate body temperature, blood pressure and blood sugar levels, declines in middle age. During our youth, these hormones help us "grow up", but the effect hormonal changes have on the aging body is still not entirely known.

What is known is that many middle-aged men experience lowered libido and reduced energy and stamina. These symptoms are mainly caused by lower levels of key male hormones such as testosterone and DHEA (dehydroepiandrosterone).

Women also experience changes in hormones before and during menopause. This is often accompanied by hot flashes, dizziness, sleeplessness and anxiety and can also be a precursor for diseases such as heart disease and osteoporosis.

Heart

Scientists are discovering that while some parts of our bodies weaken naturally as we age, others have the remarkable potential to stay in excellent condition well past the middle years. The heart is an organ that can be vigorous for as long as we live - provided we give it the care it needs.

The human heart is like the engine of a car. If it's not performing well, chances are good it hasn't been well looked after. With a healthy diet, regular aerobic exercise and by avoiding cigarettes and excess stress, an 80-year-old heart can work as well as a 20-year-old's. Taking charge of your health seems a small price to pay when you consider the returns on your investment!

Muscle Mass

Taking a brisk walk in place of watching television will only increase this investment in aging well. Exercise is vital in maintaining your heart's health along with your muscle mass. During puberty, all the muscle cells are intact and simply enlarge with use and shrink with inactivity. As you age, however, those who opt for a sedentary lifestyle will have lost roughly 25% of their muscle mass by the age of 70.

This can be turned around. In a Tufts University study, 10 frail men and women worked out with free weights for two months and the result was an increase of thigh muscle strength of 174% and muscle mass by 9%. By making a lifelong commitment to weight-bearing exercise and resistance training, it is thought that we can keep about 90% of our muscle mass well into old age.

Brain

Before the image of a healthy body and a vacant mind finds its way into your imagination, let me assure you that there are many ways to make sure your brain stays sharp. It won't surprise you to learn that mentally active people stay alert even as they grow old. There can be a little short-term memory loss and a slower reaction time as messages take a little longer to travel down nerve pathways. This likely won't show up until age 70 and could mean you answer questions a little more slowly but no less competently.

Skin

It's not shocking that years on this planet means your skin takes a beating. It's your body's first line of defense against pollution and it will become less healthy as you age. Normally aged skin shows thinning, a loss of elasticity and the deepening of normal expression lines. If you've had excess sun, or have been a long-time smoker or drinker, your skin will tell that story quite honestly to the world with wrinkles, spots and a yellowed, rough and leathery appearance. You can be smug about your age if you like, but your skin will tell the truth. Like other organs in the body, the skin needs both internal and external nourishment and tender loving care.

Immune System

Now what about the immune system? Our immune system does become less

Did You Know...

People in their late nineties or older are often healthier and more robust than those 20 years younger

Did You Know...

As the body ages, the liver and kidney's ability to cleanse toxins and metabolize most drugs decreases.

efficient as we age. It's often too weak to effectively fend off disease and is more likely to react to innocent substances or even attack itself as we see in auto-immune diseases.

The good news is, we have learned about many things that can help strengthen and support the immune system well into old age.

Optimizing Health - At Any Age

Yes, it's true some of your physical functions will slow down or change in some way. Fortunately, there are many things you can do to ensure that you are, in fact, getting better rather than getting older. Here are some suggestions for optimizing your health - no matter what your age.

Any anti-aging program needs to start with a good diet as a foundation since over-eating or eating the wrong things can be a source of body pollution and part of an age-acceleration process as well. So keep an eye both on quality and quantity of the food you eat. Choose highly nutritious foods that meet but don't exceed your daily calorie requirements. Following my guidelines for a healthy diet and referring to the Lifestyle Pyramid will ensure that you're eating to maximize your health and vitality for the rest of your life.

When it comes to food and aging, less is more. It was first noted in the 1930's that a low-calorie diet almost doubled the maximum life span of laboratory rats. Calorie-restricted animals are also more youthful in appearance, mentally quicker and physiologically younger than normally fed animals. These experiments have been conducted in short-lived species where results can be obtained within months or just a few years. The big question is whether calorie restriction has the same benefits for humans - preliminary research suggests it does.

Fast Fact

Gerontologists generally believe that the maximum life span is greater than 85 years and may, in fact, be closer to 120 years.

Studies such as the Biosphere 2 experiments mentioned in Chapter One have shown that humans react similarly to other species on a calorie-restricted nutritional program. If this is true, it is hypothesized that human lifespan may also be extended similarly to animal models.

Supplements Can Help

While diet and even calorie restriction can have great benefits as you age, alone they are not enough. You also need age-specific nutritional supplements to boost your level of nutrients. Included at the end of this chapter is a chart which outlines anti-aging supplements and the benefits they provide.

There is an army of supplements that specifically help alleviate or prevent many of the problems associated with aging and improve quality of life. Many of these have been discussed in previous chapters and are outlined in the charts throughout this book.

Let's look at a few in detail as they relate to aging:

- Several anti-oxidants have been shown to help with age-related conditions. Blueberries for instance have been recognized for their ability to reverse short-term memory loss and forestall other effects of aging.

- Vitamin E, C and zinc are known to delay the progression of macular degeneration, the leading cause of blindness in aging adults. Zinc also helps boost immune function, and is a mineral many older people are deficient in.

- Calcium, magnesium and vitamin D can prevent bone loss experienced by many aging women.

- Ginkgo Biloba helps improve circulation to the brain and extremities. Its antioxidant actions benefit the brain, retina of the eye, and the cardiovascular system. In addition to this, Ginkgo Biloba exerts a protective effect on the cells of the nervous system.

Did You Know...

As we age, our ability to absorb nutrients decreases significantly - supplements that assist with absorption can help.

Fast Fact

Ginkgo Biloba is among the leading prescription medicines in Germany and France.

- Evening Primrose oil is particularly recommended for dry and devitalized skin. It has moisturizing, nourishing and restructuring properties thanks to its high unsaturated fatty acid content. The oil helps to reduce signs of aging.

• Goldenseal is considered by contemporary herbalists to be antiseptic and astringent and recommended for many age-related skin conditions.

Anti-Aging - Women

Like Cleopatra, who used specially made ointments to enhance her appearance or Queen Elizabeth I whose remedies helped cover her smallpox scars, women from every culture in the world have been using herbal concoctions since the beginning of time to help them look and feel younger. While some of these herbal remedies have been replaced with a modern equivalent, others have stood the test of time and remain as effective today as they were centuries ago.

Health Tip

Regular exercise and optimal calcium intake are the two best ways to maximize bone strength and avoid osteoporosis

Dong Quai

One of these, dong quai (sometimes known as dang-gui), is often referred to as the female ginseng and is traditionally used to quell the hot flashes often associated with menopause.

This versatile herb has a distinguished history in the Orient and is often used as a female tonic. It's known to have a very balancing effect on women's hormonal cycles and can be especially helpful during times of hormonal upheaval. It also helps to restore menstrual regularity and regulate the reproductive system.

Black Cohosh

Another amazing herb is black cohosh, popular in Germany for treating hot flashes. Black cohosh has substances that bind to estrogen receptors in animal studies, helping to naturally regulate hormone levels. It also lowers luteinizing hormone (a hormone which is elevated in menopause) in humans. Black cohosh was an official drug in the U.S. Pharmacopoeia from 1820 to 1926.

Soy

Soybeans and soy products are recommended by nutritionists and traditional, as well as homeopathic doctors because of the high content of phytoestrogens. Phytoestrogens are natural plant estrogens that have a beneficial, neutralizing affect on female hormone levels. A diet rich in soy isoflavones decreases hot flashes, depression, moodiness and sleeplessness. Studies at Bowman Gray Medical School indicated that the consumption of 30 to 40 grams of soy per day lowered blood pressure and cholesterol. Additional research at the University of Illinois showed increased bone density. Soy is also recommended for breast cancer prevention. In addition, the U.S. FDA has backed a health claim which states that 25g of soy per day can be an effective tool to battle heart disease.

Red Clover

Red clover is also used to treat conditions associated with menopause, such as hot flashes, cardiovascular health and the bone-loss associated with osteoporosis. It contains similar compounds to those in soy - known as isoflavones. Isoflavones have been found to be effective in treating a variety of conditions.

Anti-Aging - Men

Maca

Over the ages, men have been concerned with maintaining vitality, stamina and virility. It was Peruvian shepherds, rather than scientists, who made an exciting discovery. For centuries, the botanical maca root has grown wild in the Peruvian Andes just below the glacial icecap. The only area where this particular species of maca is found is a region of extreme weather conditions such as freezing, high winds and intensive sunlight. No other food plant exists in the world which can grow at such a high altitude.

Native shepherds observed that the herds who fed on maca were healthier, had more energy and became much more sexually active. Soon the Andean people included maca in their diets and experienced similar results.

Traditionally, maca has been used as an aphrodisiac in men and to treat impotence and erectile dysfunction. It's also been used to increase endurance in athletes, promote mental clarity, and improve male fertility. According to sixth and seventh century chronicles, the Inca troops were fed maca because it was believed to give vitality and physical strength to the warriors.

Fast Fact

By 2030, about 20 percent of the population is expected to be 65 or over as compared to about 12 percent in 1990.

Tribulus

Another popular folk medicine remedy is tribulus. Ancient Greeks used the dried fruits of the plant as a general tonic. In India, it's been used as an aphrodisiac and the Chinese use it in liver, kidney, urinary and cardiovascular remedies. Historically, the most common use of this plant is for treating sexual dysfunction. Empirical evidence suggests that tribulus successfully treated impotence and improved libido.

In recent years, these cross-cultural findings piqued the interest of scientists at the Chemical Pharmaceutical Research Institute in Bulgaria, who looked at tribulus as an alternative to pharmaceutical treatments for infertility and other reproductive disorders. By 1981, standardized tribulus extracts had entered into mainstream Eastern European medical practice as a treatment for low libido, infertility and poor sexual functions.

Protein Extracts (Amino Acids)

Another of nature's anti-aging miracles is L-Lysine, an essential amino acid that enhances bone density and immune function. Amino acids are the building blocks that make proteins which maintain the functional stability of cells and tissues. Many amino acids are even more essential as we get older to ensure that proteins are strong and continue to rebuild themselves. Certain amino acids gently and naturally raise hormone levels in the male body. This offsets some of the negative factors of hormone reduction during aging without the side effects of hormone therapy drugs.

L-Arginine is an important amino acid found in collagen protein. It stimulates the release of the growth hormone needed for the proper functioning of the immune system. Growth hormone can help the body burn fat and develop lean muscle mass. L-Arginine is also excellent in promoting wound healing and bone repair.

L-Lysine, taken in combination with L-Arginine was proven in a study conducted at the University of Rome, Italy, to be much more effective. Tests show that these two amino acids together improve cell function and growth. This combination also has anti-aging benefits and assists in the healthy functioning of the immune system. L-Lysine is a necessary protein building block and helps calcium absorption.

Another amino acid, L-Glutamine, is the most abundant amino acid in muscle tissue. L-Glutamine supplementation may help maximize muscle growth. In a recent study, it caused a significant increase in growth-hormone levels.

Conclusion

Every phase of life presents enormous challenges and aging is no different. Think of being on an exercise treadmill and turning up the pace a little. Now think of getting older in the same way. To some extent, in order to stay young and active, you're swimming against the current. The pace has increased in the sense that looking after yourself will require more vigilance and care than it did when you were in your twenties. But the current increases very gradually and by adapting to it as you go along, you'll stay well ahead of the crowd.

You have lots of allies in your battle against premature aging. A healthy diet (based on our lifestyle pyramid) is fundamental to maintaining health and vigor over the long haul. Supplements take on an ever greater importance in this stage of life as they fight the accumulated effects of body pollution.

Now that you're knowledgeable about the many ways to stay young and the supplements that are now widely available to assist you in your quest for vibrancy and vitality, you too will join those few who serve as an inspiration to others.

Take Action Today

1. *Even if you don't need to lose weight, limit your total calorie intake to prevent premature aging.*

2. *Use nutritional supplements daily as outlined to delay or prevent age related conditions.*

3. *Exercise regularly, focusing on weight bearing exercises to maintain muscle mass and aerobic exercise to help burn fat.*

Table 10-1: Aging Chart

Herb	Active Ingredients	Action in Body	Focus of Current Research /Traditional Use	Antioxidant Properties
Avena Sativa	Avenine, Avenacosides	Calming effect, Aphrodisiac	High Cholesterol, Heart Health, Anxiety, Eczema, Sexual Enhancement	
Black Cohosh	Isoflavones, Triterpene glycosides	Natural Hormone Regulation	Menopausal Symptoms, Dysmenorrhea (painful menstruation), Osteoporosis	
Catuaba	Alkaloids, Phytosterols, Aromatic oils	Tonic, Antibacterial, Antiviral	Aphrodisiac, Male Sexual Health, Fatigue	
Chaste Tree Berry	Flavonoids, Iridoid glycosides, Terpenoids	Natural hormone regulation	Dysmenorrhea (painful menstruation) Premenstrual Syndrome	✓
Cranberry	Proanthocyanidins	Anti-bacterial (adherence)	Urinary tract infection	
Dong Quai	Coumarins, Ferulic Acid, Polysaccharides, Volatile Oils,	Natural hormone regulator, Muscle relaxant, Adaptogen	Dysmenorrhea (painful menstruation), Menopause, Premenstrual syndrome	
Epimedium Grandiflorum	Polysaccharides, Flavonoids, Sterols	Tonic, Natural hormone regulator	Aphrodisiac, Male Sexual Health, Blood Pressure, Aging	✓
Evening Primrose	Essential Fatty Acids	Skin Health, Natural hormone regulation	Eczema, Skin conditions, Diabetes, Premenstrual Syndrome, Osteoporosis	
Ginkgo Biloba	Flavonoglycosides, Lactones, Ginkgolides, Bilobalides	Increase circulation, Nerve Cell Protection	Age-related cognitive decline (ARCD), Alzheimer's disease, Macular Degeneration, Diabetes, Memory	✓
Goldenseal	Isoquinoline Alkaloids	Antimicrobial, Immune Support	Skin infections, Problem skin, Common cold	✓
Gotu Kola	Saponins, Flavonoids, Volatile Oil	Promote wound healing, Prevent scar formation	Burns, Scarring, Varicose Veins, Wound Healing	
L-Arginine		Wound healing, Cleansing (ammonia), Immune Support, Natural hormone regulation	Heart Health, Infertility (male), Athletic Performance, Male Sexual Health, High blood pressure	
L-Glutamine		Energy, Immune Function, Anti-inflammatory	Infection, Ulcer, HIV support	✓

Herb	Active Ingredients	Action in Body	Focus of Current Research /Traditional Use	Antioxidant Properties
L-Lysine		Maintenance & growth, Nitrogen balance	Osteoporosis, Muscle growth and tone	
Maca	Alkaloids, Saponins, Sterols, Glucosinolates	Energy, Immune Function,Tonic	Fatigue, Infertility (male), Aphrodisiac, Stamina, Athletic Endurance	
Muira Puama	Alkaloids, Coumarin, Muirapuamine	Tonic Nervous System Support	Male Sexual Health Stamina Endurance	
Nettle	Polysaccharides, Lectins, Sterols	Anti-inflammatory, Diuretic,Tonic,	Urinary Tract Infection, Benign Prostatic Hyperplasia, Hay fever, Rheumatoid Arthritis, Skin Conditions	
Panax Ginseng	Ginsenosides, Panaxins, Polysaccharides	Energy,Immune FunctionTonic,	Diabetes,Infection, Athletic PerformanceInfertility, Chronic Fatigue Syndrome, Cancer Prevention	
Pygeum Africanum	Ferulic Acid, Phytosterols	Prostatic health	Benign prostatic hyperplasia	
Red Clover Leaf	Isoflavones, Coumarins	Blood Purifier,Natural hormone regulator	Psoriasis, Eczema,Cancer risk reduction, Menopausal Symptoms	
Red Raspberry	Gallic and Egallic Acids	Muscle Relaxant, Anti-nausea	Painful Menstruation, Morning Sickness	
Tribulus Terrestris	Saponins	Natural hormone regulator	Male Sexual Health	

CHAPTER **11**

Stress and Exercise

You're caught in a traffic jam, your cell phone is on the fritz, you're already late for an important 9 a.m. meeting at your office, you're starting to hyperventilate and your stomach's in knots. By the time you rush in at 9:20, you're so exhausted; you'd like to be ending your day, not starting it. What all this stress and anxiety does to you internally, you really don't want to know. Or maybe you do, because only when you know what's happening to your body can you begin to control or at least manage stress.

You've just experienced the same reaction your caveman ancestor had after being threatened by a raging animal (or other human). The difference is that he would have run away or fought to defend himself - what is known as the 'fight or flight' reaction. The caveman would never have heard of 'stress' - it's a modern-day phenomenon. Today we have the same adrenaline coursing through our bodies but seldom the opportunity to work it off physically.

It's as if adrenaline were a kind of acid that supercharged your body's batteries. Just what you need for any occasion that requires super-human strength or to make a quick getaway. If your situation is psychologically rather than physically stressful, that same 'acid' causes internal damage over time.

Stress, as I'm sure you know from personal experience, takes a huge toll on the body, especially when it's re-created day after day on a long-term basis. Work for someone you don't get along with? You probably don't even notice the anxiety buildup on a daily basis. Maybe you've gotten used to it, but it's ticking away, robbing you of energy and also of your youthfulness. Whatever happened to that great disposition you used to have? And the way you used to fall asleep so easily?

By taking a close look at stress, you can find ways to reduce it in your life and also learn ways to manage the kinds of stress that you just may have to live with. You can even find ways to make it work for you rather than against you. Let's start at the beginning with a definition.

What is Stress?

Stress is basically the "wear and tear" our bodies experience as we adjust to our continually changing environment; it has physical and emotional effects on us that can be either positive or negative. On the positive side, stress can give us the motivation and strength to get through difficult situations. On the negative side, stress can diminish our emotional and physical well-being.

Work deadlines, family concerns, pain, traffic jams, economic pressures, as well as job promotions, new homes and marriages are some of the many sources of stress affecting us on a daily basis. Even very positive changes in our life can be taxing. Change itself is stressful. Not to change is also stressful. There's no avoiding it - we need to learn to deal with it!

Types of Stress

Survival Stress:

- When your survival or health is threatened or if you're put under pressure or experience some unpleasant or challenging event.
- Your body releases adrenaline and you experience the 'fight or flight' reaction.

Internally Generated Stress:

- Anxious worrying about events beyond your control; a tense, hurried approach to life or relationship problems.
- Can also result from an 'addiction to stress' or actual enjoyment and drive from being stressed.

Environmental and Job Stress:

- Stressful living or working environment.
- It may come from noise, crowding, pollution, untidiness, conflict or other distractions.
- Deadlines, presentations, job security are other forms of job stress.

Fatigue and Overwork:

- Here stress builds up over a long period - chronic stress can occur when you try to achieve too much in too little time or if you're not using effective time management strategies.

Fast Fact

75% of the general population experiences at least some stress every two weeks.

Stress as Body Pollution

Back in caveman days, stress occurred on occasion and was literally a matter of life and death. The body was challenged, responded physically and was then given time to rest and recover. Today, stress has become a part of everyday life and we are in chronic states of "alert" so much of the time, we've come to think of this condition as normal. Stress has become our constant companion.

When we suffer from chronic stress by worrying about a sick family member or losing a job, stress hormones are produced in high levels over long periods of time and they start to exhaust the body's resources to deal with it. Stress then becomes a form of body pollution.

Sharon doesn't get along with her boss. Going to work every morning is an ordeal. The office building's ventilation system is malfunctioning, so she's breathing in stale air. She doesn't have time for lunch so she asks a co-worker to bring her back a burger and fries which she eats at her desk. She calls home to find that her six-year-old son's teacher wants to talk to her about his behaviour. It's just 1:15 in the afternoon and Sharon already feels exhausted.

Whew!! Makes you long for the caveman days, doesn't it? This scenario isn't as uncommon as we'd like to think. Sharon's just had a heavy dose of body pollution from a number of sources - the emotional situation at work, the air she breathes, the toxins and preservatives in the fried food she's eating (not to mention the excess calories!) and the dicey situation on the home front. If she thinks this doesn't affect her health and well-being, she's kidding herself.

When you consider that people go through similar (and worse) situations on a daily basis, you can only marvel at the resilience of the human body! By significantly reducing the stress in your life, you'll harness energy that can be expended in much more positive ways. Stress is a form of body pollution much like other toxins and while it can't be avoided entirely, you need to be aware of the negative effects and deal with them.

Did You Know...

Work stress can be as harmful to health as smoking or not exercising.

Mental stress, or simply the negative thoughts we all have from time to time, is also a kind of body pollution - perhaps we should call it mind pollution. Fuelled by media reports of the latest disaster, mind pollution can become the context for your life if you're not careful. Then life becomes stressful in and of itself. Stress also leads to bad habits such as eating disorders, (eating too much or too little) and disrupted sleep patterns. Both conditions wear you down physically over time.

Fast Fact

Tranquilizers, anti-depressants and anti-anxiety medications account for one-fourth of all prescriptions written in the U.S. each year.

The Stress Reaction

No matter what the source of stress, it causes an automatic "fight or flight" response which affects virtually all bodily processes and organs. Adrenaline rushes in, blood pressure rises and muscles tense up. In an effort to produce lots of energy quickly, the body increases its metabolism of proteins, fats and carbohydrates and excretes lots of nutrients including potassium, magnesium, calcium and amino acids. Digestion slows down which causes fats and sugars to be released from body stores, and also causes a rise in cholesterol and a decrease in the absorption of nutrients.

While you sometimes need the adrenaline that stress releases, a stressed-out body is simply not a healthy body! Under sustained stress, certain functions shut down or work less effectively - here's a summary of the stress reaction:

The Stress Reaction:

- The body/mind perceives a threat through any of its senses.
- The concerned sense organ sends a message to the brain.
- The stress hormone adrenaline is released.
- The heart beats faster, respiratory rates rise and blood pressure rises.
- The liver increases output of blood sugar.
- Blood flow is diverted away from the gastro-intestinal system to the brain and large muscles.
- The blood vessels at the extremities contract in order to increase clotting in case of cuts or wounds.
- The pupils dilate so we can see better.
- After the threat or anger passes, the body relaxes again.

The Impact of Stress on Your Health

Stress, particularly if it's prolonged and intense, can increase the risk of developing serious medical conditions and can make existing conditions worse. Stress alone rarely causes disease, but physicians say it plays a crucial role in whether the body initially resists a disease as well as how that disease subsequently runs its course.

Chronic stress can wear down your cardiovascular system, immune system and gastrointestinal system among others. It contributes to an increased risk or worsening of heart disease, migraines, asthma and several other diseases.

Fast Fact

The Confederation of British Industry estimates that businesses lost £10.2 billion in 1998 through lost productivity caused by stress.

Cancer

Studies show that stress may make you more vulnerable to a wide range of cancers and once you're ill, stress can slow down the healing process. In a recent study, breast cancer patients who experienced high levels of stress from their diagnosis and treatment had weaker immune systems than those who experienced less stress. These highly stressed women had lower levels of the natural killer cells that detect and kill cancer cells.

Heart Disease

The heart works extremely hard under stress, whether physical or mental. Your blood pressure is elevated, your blood clotting mechanism is working at full force, your heart is beating faster than normal and your metabolic rate is up. Keep it up for hours and you'll be exhausted. Keep it up for years and you could well bring on a heart attack. Stress is certainly a secondary risk factor for heart disease.

Studies of patients with coronary artery disease show that those who learn how to manage their stress along with traditional medical care significantly reduced their rate of future heart attacks compared with those who didn't.

Health Tip

Exercise can turn your body into a fat-burning machine because it continues to burn calories at an elevated rate for a minimum of 30 minutes after you exercise

Immune System

When under stress, the immune system is suppressed leaving the body vulnerable to an array of illnesses.

In one experiment, after 21 days of being stressed, lab animals' immune systems became suppressed and stopped working properly. It was as though it had been pushed too hard and needed to shut down for a rest.

Stress can even make you more susceptible to the common cold. In one study, human subjects were inoculated with strains of a virus, then quarantined and monitored. Those with higher levels of stress came down with cold symptoms.

The good news is that we are not helpless victims. Just as we can fight other types of body pollution, we can also mitigate stress's effect by taking concrete and positive action.

Stress Management

The first step is to stop a moment and acknowledge the stress in your life. In choosing the right method for you to alleviate stress, ask yourself what the source of your stress is. If outside factors such as an important upcoming event or relationship difficulties are the cause, then a positive thinking technique may be effective. The events are not in themselves stressful, it's what you tell yourself about them that causes the stress. If stress and fatigue are long-term, then lifestyle and organizational or dietary changes may be appropriate. Chances are good you'll need a combination of all these methods.

In order to manage stress in your life, you will have to do something differently that will either change the stressful situation in your life or change your attitude and reaction to it.

Here are some helpful stress reduction techniques:

1. Take deep relaxing breaths frequently throughout the day.
2. Do a body check last thing at night and first thing in the morning to find out exactly where stress is showing up in your body.
3. Focus on goal-setting and regular planning.
4. Make reading positive books a daily activity.
5. Find more opportunities to laugh - even at your troubles!

6. Avoid negative influences as much as possible, whether it's a co-worker, the media, television violence, etc. It's debilitating!

7. Learn to meditate or to have quiet time on a daily basis.

8. Make time for positive interactions with the people you love.

9. Spend some time each week doing what you love - dancing, singing, reading, working out, whatever it may be for you.

10. Become more physically active.

During stressful periods, it's more important than ever to eat well to maintain a healthy body. Continuous stress can deplete vitamins, especially the B-vitamins and cause electrolyte imbalances. Stress also promotes the formation of free radicals that can damage cell membranes and body tissue.

And don't forget what we learned so far about the minerals and herbs known to boost the immune system, such as zinc, astragalus, reishi mushroom and licorice root. Phytonutrients and some vitamins act as antioxidants that help control free radicals. Excellent nutrition in general, helps to combat stress and keep it under control.

Exercise

Stress and inactivity go hand in hand. We get a shot of adrenaline and we're sitting in front of our computers so we can't work it off. This is where exercise comes in. Whether our stress has situational, physical or psychological roots, exercise helps to wipe out the anxious energy that results.   Sadly, anywhere around the world, 60-85% of the population is not physically active.

Making time for physical activity is a vital link to reducing your chances of chronic disease and enhancing your potential for a fulfilled life. Years ago, people remained on their feet and active throughout the day. Life was based on physical activity.

Today as a whole, our lifestyle is much more sedentary. We sit in our cars going to and from work or school and even "drive through" banks and restaurants. At work, many of us sit behind our desks letting telephones, computers and fax machines handle the activities. At home the seductive television set and video games call out for our attention.

We don't even have to get up to adjust the volume or change the channel. We've simply stopped moving. And we've come to accept all this as normal.

Health Tip

Circuit weight training (moving continuously between different exercise machines) combines the best of aerobic exercise and weight training - it is one of the best overall exercise programs.

Our stress levels have nowhere to go but inward if we spend too much time sitting down. We can look forward to the theatre and bus seats expanding another four inches in the next ten years so they can accommodate us. It's not surprising that many of us are overweight and out of breath at the slightest exertion. We're passing on a toxic lifestyle to our children who are gaining weight at a phenomenal rate.

Sedentary Children

"There is deep concern over the fitness of American youth." It is so shocking that U.S. News and World Report published a special 11 page section warning the nation.

"Parents are being warned that their children - taken to schools in buses, chauffeured to activities, freed from muscle-building chores and entertained in front of TV sets - are getting soft and flabby."

Recent article in the newspaper? Well, it could be but this article was published on August 2nd, 1957. And it was right on. Too bad we ignored the writing on the wall and now more than 45 years later the situation is even worse.

Childhood and physical activity used to be the norm. Most adults, no matter where they come from, remember childhood as a time of actively playing outdoors until darkness and exhaustion forced them to return home. Cold weather, rain, nothing stopped these children from doing what came naturally. And if they came home and ate a home-cooked brownie, it didn't do a lot of harm simply because they were so active on a regular basis.

Children today are much more likely to spend their free time exercising little but their fingers as they push the controls of an electronic game or switch TV channels from the couch. Of course, while children are watching television, they're reminded that they'd like another snack. Even every day calorie-burning tasks such as walking to school or riding a bike to visit a friend have been replaced by car rides.

If you or your children are in danger of not getting enough exercise, it's not hard to turn things around. The best thing is that you'll begin to see the benefits almost right away in terms of renewed energy, strength and enthusiasm for life.

Benefits of Exercise

Regular physical activity provides substantial physical, social and mental health gains. It's an outlet for stress and also protects against the risk of major chronic disease - in particular heart disease, hypertension, colon cancer, diabetes and osteoporosis - let's have a closer look.

Stress Reduction

Exercise benefits those of us who battle stress daily by helping us to calm down and work off tensions. And over time, some experts contend, people who exercise regularly develop a more efficient biochemical mechanism for handling life's pressures - a kind of 'stress resistance'.

This 'tension-busting' effect is really important in our modern stressed-out society where an estimated 60-90% of all physician visits are for stress-related complaints such as headache, backache, muscle tension, insomnia, anxiety, arthritis and depression - to name just a few.

While stress releases 'stress' hormones, exercise seems to have a calming effect. When you exercise, the body produces substances called endorphins which naturally relieve pain and induce feelings of well-being and relaxation. They have a similar chemical structure to morphine and are also released during laughter.

Heart Disease and Cholesterol

Active people have a 45% lower risk of developing heart disease than do sedentary people. Moderate dietary changes improve cholesterol levels and lower the risk for coronary artery disease more successfully when an aerobic program (exercise that increases the heart rate) is followed. Regular aerobic exercises - brisk walking, jogging, swimming, biking, dance and racquet sports - are the best forms of exercise for lowering LDL (bad cholesterol) and raising HDL (good cholesterol) cholesterol levels.

Did You Know...

Nearly half of all young people ages 12-21 aren't vigorously active on a regular basis.

Fast Fact

A fit heart pumps 25% more blood per minute when at rest and over 60% more blood per minute during physical exertion than an unfit heart.

High Blood Pressure

Regular exercise helps keep arteries elastic, even in older people and this keeps blood flowing and blood pressure low. Sedentary people have a 35% greater risk of developing hypertension than active people do.

Health
Tip

Power walking (walking at a very rapid pace while pumping your arms) is an exercise everyone can do - it improves cardiovascular health and helps the body burn fat.

Diabetes

Aerobic exercise is proving to have significant and particular benefits for people with both type 1 and type 2 diabetes. It increases the body's ability to use insulin, lowers blood pressure, improves cholesterol levels and decreases body fat.

Osteoporosis

Exercise slows the progress of osteoporosis. People should begin exercising before adolescence, since bone mass increases during puberty and reaches its peak between ages 20 and 30. Weight bearing exercise, which applies tension to muscle and bone, encourages the body to compensate for the added stress and can increase bone density by as much as 2% to 8% a year.

Cancer

You may be shocked to know that a number of studies indicate that regular, even moderate, exercise reduces the risk of colon cancer. Strenuous activity, in fact, adds only slight or no additional benefit. There is also scientific evidence that a regular program of physical activity may help in preventing several hormonally-related cancers including breast, endometrial, prostate, and testicular cancer.

Psychological and Emotional Benefits

Aerobic exercise is linked with improved mental vigor, including reaction time, acuity and math skills. Exercising may even enhance creativity and imagination. According to one study, older people who are physically fit respond to mental challenges just as quickly as unfit young adults.

Exercise and Weight Loss

Earlier, I pointed out the risks involved with the alarming rise of overweight people. Obesity is now an epidemic and physical inactivity is one of the leading reasons. Calorie restriction is important but exercise is the second essential component.

One of exercise's key benefits is that it raises the metabolism and burns calories five to seven times more than when resting. Better still, the accelerated metabolism stays that way for some time after exercise. This is why many experts recommend going for a brisk pre-breakfast walk to get the metabolism revved up for the day.

Exercise won't always show up on your weight scales, since it turns fatty tissue into lean muscle tissue and muscle actually weighs more than fat. It will show up in your body's shape though, and you'll soon find your clothes beginning to fit you better. Not to mention an improved posture. For these reasons alone, regular exercise is a great way to stay looking young. Scales are not the only measure!

While aerobic exercise gets your heart and lungs working out, you also need weight training. Muscle is a dynamic tissue that requires more calories to maintain than fat tissue. As a result, adding muscle tissue will increase your resting metabolic rate (the pace at which calories are burned) and enhance the likelihood of long-term weight maintenance. Since your metabolic rate accounts for 60-75% of your daily energy expenditure, increasing your metabolism with both aerobic and strength training exercises will help you burn more calories during all of your activities, including sleep!

So you can feel really virtuous if you sleep in on the weekend, knowing that your metabolism is working on your behalf!

Exercise and Aging

As you get older, you gain weight, become much less mobile, suffer from arthritis and slowly stop activities such as dancing, biking, swimming, right? Wrong! While this is reality for many people, it really almost always boils down to choice and if you don't choose to begin shutting your life down at a certain point, chances are good you won't have to. You'll remain active as long as you live.

A lot of the decline and physical problems that go along with aging have more to do with inactivity than it does with getting older. Regular exercise can help people stay healthy, active and independent as they age. People who eat well, exercise regularly and take nutritional supplements can drop 10 to 20 years from their biological age. Sounds good to me!

Did You Know...

According to the World Health Organization approximately 2 million deaths per year are attributed to physical inactivity.

Let's quickly review the many benefits of exercise:

Did You Know...

- Reduces the risk of premature death.
- Helps control weight.
- Helps control diabetic blood glucose levels.
- Helps control blood pressure.
- Helps control blood cholesterol levels by increasing good cholesterol levels (HDL).
- Helps build healthy bones, muscles and joints (prevents osteoporosis).
- Reduces feelings of depression and anxiety.
- Reduces the risk of colon cancer.
- Helps older adults become stronger with greater mobility.
- Improves blood circulation and helps the heart, lungs and other organs and muscles work together more effectively.
- Promotes psychological well-being.
- Helps relieve stress.

Wow! Can you believe all the benefits? And it won't cost you a cent!

What are you waiting for? Start lacing up those roller blades. Or at least begin walking up the stairs instead of taking the elevator. It's never too late to begin reaping the benefits of regular exercise.

Adding Exercise to Your Life

For the greatest overall health benefits, experts recommend at least 20 to 30 minutes of aerobic activity three or more times a week along with some type of stretching and muscle-strengthening activity. This may seem a little daunting for those of us who aren't used to exercising or aren't the "athletic" type but there are easy and fun ways to incorporate activity into your life.

Choose an activity you enjoy. Whether that's going to the gym, a yoga class or a brisk after-dinner walk - the important thing is to make it part of your daily routine. Many of us can't fit large chunks of time for exercise into our busy schedules. If you find setting aside a half-hour a day is tough, start making changes to your every day activities to incorporate physical activity. Five minutes of activity here and there will soon add up to your recommended thirty minutes and become second nature.

Fast Fact

The American Council on Exercise reports that a 120-pound woman who walks for 30 minutes at a speedy 12-minute-mile pace (that's practically a jog for many of us) will burn 195 calories, while a 140-pound woman walking at the same rate will burn 228 calories.

Here are a few examples of how you can easily begin to introduce exercise into your life:

• Parking the car at the far end of the parking lot.
• Gardening, raking leaves and mowing the lawn.
• Housework such as cleaning, vacuuming, dusting etc.
• Using stairs and walking whenever possible rather than using elevators, escalators and moving sidewalks.
• Walking during lunch breaks.
• Using fewer labour-saving devices such as remote controls.
• Playing with or babysitting toddlers or young children.

Did You Know...

Physical inactivity is as strong an independent risk factor for lifestyle related diseases as smoking and an unhealthy diet

Conclusion

In this chapter, we've looked at two critical components of good health. The effect that stress has on our health can't be overlooked, especially when many adults need help dealing with it.

Taking a positive attitude will help you deal with the inevitable stresses your life contains. Remember that what happens to you is not as important as how well you deal with it.

Remember to add exercise to your day, no matter how packed-full it already is. Exercise will actually give you time since it provides you more energy and also helps you concentrate so you can get more done in less time.

Exercise and stress reduction will help you feel great and stay healthy - these are very powerful benefits!

Take Action Today

1. *Realize that stress is a form of body pollution that weakens your immune system's ability to protect you from disease.*

2. *Incorporate some forms of stress reduction techniques into your daily life. It could be as simple as listening to relaxing music.*

3. *Exercise is vital to health. Pick an activity that you enjoy and do it as often as possible.*

CHAPTER 12

Now for a Brand New Life!

We've come to the final chapter in this book which I fervently hope will be a new chapter in your life. A new chapter where you've made a decision to become well informed about your own lifestyle choices.

You've learned about body pollution and the profound effect it has on your health. Even more importantly, you've learned how to protect yourself from it.

I'm sure we agree that we wouldn't want to exchange our modern lifestyle with all its conveniences for a completely pure environment - even if we could! We do however need to realize that we must make some serious lifestyle changes in order to live a long, healthy and active life. The fact is, these days we all have to fight for our health - we can no longer take it for granted.

Thankfully, there's lots of evidence that taking a proactive approach will not only add years to your life but also make those years more enjoyable. Who can argue with that? Not the Okinawans who eat a low-calorie, additive-free diet and have the world's largest number of centarians. Nor the participants in Biosphere 2 with their low-calorie, nutrient-rich diet and pure atmosphere. Let these two groups serve as inspiration and perfect examples - showing you that it is possible to transform your life. Applying the principles in this book will show you how to do just that - without leaving the city you live in!

Below I've listed the key concepts from each chapter along with a summary of the 'Take Action Todays' in a convenient step-by-step format. I must emphasize that every one of these steps is important. It won't do to get all the exercise you need and yet ignore your body's nutritional requirements. Neither will taking a daily vitamin be enough just by itself. There is no one magic bullet, but it's important to start somewhere. The more positive steps you can take against body pollution the better. You don't need to do this all at once or in any particular order. Begin with small steps, following our 'Take Action Today' guidelines and keep adding new steps until your life has been totally transformed. Incorporating all of the action steps will provide you with an almost foolproof recipe for a healthy, active life. Once you begin, you'll be amazed at how easy each step is and how much better you feel after doing it.

So what are you waiting for? Staying healthy in an unhealthy world is within your reach - Start fighting body pollution today!

Step One: Identify and inform yourself about body pollution

Inadequate diet, food additives, saturated fat and excess sodium, exposure to environmental and occupational pollutants, excessive alcohol, smoking, drug use, overeating, negative thoughts and poor drinking water are all sources of the body pollution that affects absolutely everyone who lives on this planet. Rich or poor, privileged or not, no one who breathes, eats and drinks can avoid body pollution and no one can control it, but we can all take steps to protect ourselves against it.

- Reduce your use of chemicals around the home - common sources include lawn and garden chemicals and home cleaning products.
- Be a responsible car owner and leave your car at home when you can. Look into alternative means of transportation.
- Do your part in protecting the environment by recycling as much as possible

Step Two: Realize how body pollution impacts your health

Body pollution can and does impact every aspect of your health. It can lead to a diminished enjoyment of life, accelerated aging, and chronic disease. Thanks to our modern way of life, we must be prepared to make changes to our current lifestyles so we can continue to enjoy optimal health in our beautiful but increasingly polluted world.

- Become aware of what you put in your body - ask yourself "is this contributing to body pollution"?

- Realize that being healthy and active well into old age is a reality and that illness and disease don't have to be a part of living.
- Commit to learning about lifestyle changes that can help you take control of your health and fight body pollution.

Step Three: Follow the 'Fighting Body Pollution Lifestyle Pyramid'

Diet has changed in the past 150 years but our bodies haven't. We need to provide our bodies with the building blocks needed to maintain optimal health. Quality, unrefined whole foods, rich in nutrients along with supplements, are fundamental in the battle against body pollution.

- Revamp your daily diet according to the Fighting Body Pollution Lifestyle Pyramid.
- Go through your cupboards and throw out your junk food. Read the ingredients first - can you believe you actually ate that stuff?
- Drink plenty of purified water - hydration is important in the body's cleansing process.

Step Four: Take a multivitamin and mineral supplement daily

Vitamins and minerals are essential for millions of intricate body processes. What we've now learned is that they play a major role, not only in disease prevention but in delaying disease progression. Modern food production and soil depletion don't allow us to get the full complement of vitamins and minerals needed to fight body pollution -a supplement is essential for maintaining optimal health.

- Begin taking a multi-vitamin and mineral supplement daily - base your buying decision on our tips.
- Take your vitamin and mineral supplement with food containing protein to maximize absorption.
- Be sure that your supplement meets your age and gender specific needs.

Step Five: Go back to your roots - add herbs to your daily diet

Roots, leaves, barks and berries - herbs or botanicals were once a part of our every day diet. Modern nutrition is missing these nutrients. Botanicals can support the systems of the body, giving us the strength and health to fight body pollution.

- Use herbs daily to support and strengthen the body in the fight against body pollution.

- Whenever possible, use standardized herbal supplements to ensure a consistent level of active compounds.
- Refer to the enclosed chart to use specific herbs for specific health issues.

Step Six: Eat a minimum of 5 servings of fruits and vegetables everyday

Fruits and vegetables contain a host of disease-fighting phytonutrients. Yet very few people manage to eat a variety of fruits and vegetables on a daily basis. Plant nutrients are natural compounds found in the foods we have eaten for centuries and research is now showing that these phytonutrients provide a multitude of benefits, some of which are just becoming known. Phytonutrients are a strong ally in the fight against body pollution. Make sure you get lots of them.

- For the maximum in protection from body pollution, choose fruits and vegetables with the highest ORAC (antioxidant) value as outlined in our chart.
- Supplement your daily diet with a high-quality fruit and vegetable extract supplement - ideally one with additional antioxidant vitamins and minerals added.
- Clean all fruits and vegetables of residues with a non-toxic detergent.

Step Seven: Increase your intake of dietary fibre

It seems fibre just doesn't get the press that it should. Once thought of as a throw-away product for animal feed, we are now learning that fibre does much more than just keep us 'regular.' Fibre helps to cleanse the body of toxins, is a major player in the prevention of many chronic diseases and is an essential component in weight loss programs. Give it the credit it deserves - add more fibre to your diet.

- Start adding more fibre-rich foods to your diet to help fight body pollution and cleanse your digestive system.
- Eat a wide variety of fibre foods to ensure you're getting the health benefits of both soluble and insoluble fibre.
- Add a high-fibre supplement to your diet to make sure you're reaching the recommended daily intake of 25-35 grams (for adults).

Step Eight: Control your caloric intake - eat quality, not quantity

Obesity has become a global epidemic. For the first time ever, more than 50% of the world's population is overweight - and this number is rising daily. Increased body fat is linked to a host of chronic diseases and is a major storage site for body pollution. Worse, fat tends to perpetuate itself - as we get heavier, exercise - or even movement - becomes more difficult and calorie-burning becomes inefficient as the metabolism slows down.

- Think of excess calories as a form of body pollution - consume only as many calories as you need to maintain your present weight or less to lose weight.

- Follow the Lifestyle Pyramid in Chapter 3 and you will be assured a nutrient-rich, balanced diet that focuses on quality not quantity.

- Use meal replacements and botanical supplements to help you lose weight faster.

Step Nine: Start now and reap the benefits later

No matter how old you are, you've got aging ahead of you, that is the common thread every living being shares. Regardless of your current age, the action you take now will affect how you live later. Start fighting body pollution now to stay young - at any age!

- Even if you do not need to lose weight, limit your total calorie intake to prevent premature aging.

- Use nutritional supplements daily as outlined to delay or prevent age related conditions.

- Exercise regularly, focusing on weight bearing exercises to maintain muscle mass.

Step Ten: Get Moving!

Exercise and state of mind provide invaluable benefits with no cost. How many things in life can you say that about? It does require a commitment though. Being physically active is an excellent outlet for much of the stress we hold onto day after day. Strengthening and training the body to be in top condition provides unparalleled defense against chronic disease and body pollution.

- Realize that stress is a form of body pollution and weakens your immune systems ability to protect you from disease.

- Incorporate some forms of stress reduction techniques into your daily life. It could be as simple as listening to relaxing music.

- Exercise is vital to health. Pick an activity that you enjoy and do it as often as you can.

References

Chapter One

1. Rea, William J., *Journal of Nutritional and Environmental Medicine* 1996; 6:55-124.
2. *World Health Organization*, September 2000; Guidelines for Air Pollution Control; Fact sheet No. 187
3. Eric Pianin, Washington Post Staff Writer; *Washington Post*; Wednesday, March 13, 2002; Page A08
4. Roy L. Walford et al; *Journal of Gerontology* 2002; 57A-6, B211-B224

Chapter Two

1. *American Academy of Environmental Medicine*
2. William Booth, Washington Post Staff Writer; *Washington Post*; Friday, February 1, 2002; Page A02
3. *Environmental Health Perspectives* Vol. 104 Supplement 4 (August, 1996), pgs. 807-808.
4. Crinnion, WJ., *Altern Med Rev* 2000; 5(1):52-63.
5. 1998 Cancer Facts and Figures, *American Cancer Society*
6. Levy, D., *Circulation* 1999; 100(20):2054-9.

Chapter Three

1. Whitney, EN., Rolfes, SR.; *Understanding Nutrition* 7th Edition 1996; West Publishing Company
2. Schroeder, HA. *American Journal of Clinical Nutrintion* 1971; 24(5):562-73
3. *Globe and Mail*, July 9, 2001; A1
4. Holub, B., Professor of Nutritional Sciences, University of Guelph, Canada; *Globe and Mail*, July 9th, 2002; p.R5

5. Schlosser, E; Fast food nation 2002; Houghton Mifflin
6. Martin Collins, Fitness Expert, *Globe and Mail*; July 9th, 2002; p. R5

Chapter Four

1. Bendich, A. et al, *Western J Medicine* 1997; 166:306-312
2. Boushey, CJ et al, *Journal of the American Medical Association* 1995; 274: 1049-1057
3. Fairfield, K et al, *Journal of the American Medical Association* 2002; 287(23) :3116-3162
4. Fletcher, R et al, *Journal of the American Medical Association* 2002; 287(23) :3127-3129
5. Knekt P, Heliovaara M, Aho K, et al. *Epidemiology* 2000;11:402-5.
6. Rimm EB, Stampfer MJ, Ascherio A, et al. *New England Journal of Medicine* 1993; 328: 1450-6.
7. Stephens NG, Parsons A, Schofield PM, et al. *Lancet* 1996;347:781-6.
8. Wilkinson IB, Megson IL, MacCallum H, et al. *J Cardiovasc Pharmacol* 1999;34:690-3.
9. Valkonen MM, Kuusi T. *Free Radic Biol Med* 2000 Feb 1;28(3):428-36.
10. Taylor A. *J Am Coll Nutr* 1993;12:138-46
11. Taylor A, Jacques PF, Nadler D, et al. *Curr Eye Res* 1991;10:751-9.
12. Simon JA, Hudes ES. *Journal of the American Medical Association* 1999; 281:2289-93.
13. Levine M, Rumsey SC, Daruwala R, et al. *Journal of the American Medical Association* 1999;281:1415-23.
14. Carr AC, Frei B. *Am J Clin Nutr* 1999;69:1086-107
15. Omenn GS, Goodman GE, Thornquist MD, et al. *New England Journal of Medicine* 1996;334:1150-5.
16. Neuman I, Nahum H, Ben-Amotz A. Ann *Allerg Asthma Immunol* 1999;82:549-53.
17. www.healthnotes.com
18. Lieberman, S. and Bruning, N., *The Real Vitamin and Mineral Book* 1990; Avery Publishing Group Inc.

Chapter Five

1. Whitney, EN., Rolfes, SR.; *Understanding Nutrition* 7th Edition 1996; West Publishing Company
2. Lieberman, S. and Bruning, N., *The Real Vitamin and Mineral Book* 1990; Avery Publishing Group Inc.
3. Osborne CG, McTyre RB, Dudek J, et al. *Nutr Rev* 1996;54:365-81

4. Bell L, Halstenson CE, Halstenson CJ, et al. *Arch Intern Med* 1992;152:2441-4.
5. Krger MC, Horrobin DF. *Prog Lipid Res* 1997;36:131-51
6. Mossad SB, Macknin ML, Medendorp SV, et al. Ann *Int Med* 1996;125: 81-8
7. Garland ML, Hagmeyer KO. Ann *Pharmacother* 1998;32:93-69
8. Prasad AS. J Trace Elements *Exper Med* 1998;11:63-87.
9. Clark, LC et al. *Journal of the American Medical Association* 1996 Dec 25;276(24):1957-63.
10. Peretz A, Néve J, Desmedt J, et al. *Am J Clin Nutri* 1991;53:1323-8.
11. Yoshida M, Fukunaga K, Tsuchita H, Yasumoto K. *J Nutr Sci Vitaminol* 1999;45:119-28.
12. Kawano Y, Matsuoka H, Takishita S, Omae T. *Hypertension* 1998;32: 260-5
13. Cox IM, Campbell MJ, Dowson D. *Lancet* 1991;337:757-60.
14. www.healthnotes.com
15. Firshein, R. *The Nutraceutical Revolution* 1998; The Berkley Publishing Group.

Chapter Six

1. *Reader's Digest, Family Guide to Natural Medicine* 1993; The Reader's Digest Association
2. Ody, P., *The Complete Medicinal Herbal* 1993; Dorling Kindersley
3. Tyler, VE., *Tyler's Honest Herbal* 4th Edition 1999; The Hawthorn Herbal Press
4. Murray, MT., *The Healing Power of Herbs* 2nd Edition 1995; Prima Publishing
5. Tierra, M., *Planetary Herbology* 1992; Lotus Press
6. Wren, RC., *Potter's Newcyclopaedia of Botanical Drugs & Preparations* 1988; Potter's (Herbal Supplies) Ltd.
7. Blumenthal, M., Goldberb, A., Brinckman, *J., Herbal Medicine Expanded Commission E Monographs* 2000; Integrative Medicine Communications
8. *PDR for Herbal Medicines* 1st Edition 1998; Medical Economics Company Inc.
9. Leung, A., *Better Health with (mostly) Chinese Herbs and Foods* 1995; AYSL Corporation
10. www.healthnotes.com

Chapter Seven

1. Krebs-Smith, SM., Cook, A., Subar, AF., Cleveland, L., Friday, J., and Kahle, LL. (1996) *Archives of Pediatrics and Adolescent Medicine* 150; 81-6
2. Toniolo, P. et al., *Am J Epidemiol.* 2001 Jun 15;153(12):1142-7
3. *Vegetarian Times*, October 2001, Healthy Lifestyles, p.2
4. Giovannucci E, Ascherio A, Rimm EB, et al. *J Natl Cancer Inst* 1995;87:1767-76
5. Levy J, Bosin E, Feldman B, Giat Y, et al. *Nutr Cancer* 1995;24:257-66
6. Giovannucci E. *J Natl Cancer Inst* 1999;91:317-31.
7. Paetau I, Khachik F, Brown ED, et al. *Am J Clin Nutr* 1998;68:1187-95
8. Zhang Y, Talalay P, Cho CG, Posner GH. *Proc Natl Acad Sci* 1992;89: 2399-403
9. Hecht SS. *J Nutr* 1999;129:768S-774S
10. Wild Blueberry Association of North America
11. Pace-Asciak CR, Rounova O, Hahn SE, et al. *Clin Chim Acta* 1996;246 (1-2):163-82
12. Jang M, Cai L, Udeani GO, et al. *Science* 1997;275:218-20
13. www.healthnotes.com

Chapter Eight

1. Whitney, EN., Rolfes, SR.; *Understanding Nutrition* 7th Edition 1996; West Publishing Company
2. Albertson, et al. *J Am College Nutr.* 2001; 20:585.
3. http://www.hsph.harvard.edu/cancer/press/archives/cancer_fact.pdf
4. Hill, MJ., *Eur J Cancer Prev.* 2002 Feb;11(1):1-2

Chapter Nine

1. Evenson, B. *The Weight of the World* 2002; National Post
2. http://www.niddk.nih.gov/
3. Schlosser, E; *Fast food nation* 2002; Houghton Mifflin
4. Jacobson, MJ., Liquid Candy 1998; *Centre for Science in the Public Interest*
5. Arnold, T., A real call to action 2002; *National Post*
6. Wing RR, Marcuse MD, Blair EH, et al., *Diabetes Care* 1994;17:30.
7. Pinhas-Hamiel O et al. *J Pediatr* 1996 May;128(5 Pt 1): 608-15
8. Colditz, GA., *Am J. Clin Nutr.* 1992; 55:503-507s
9. www.starchstopper.com

Chapter Ten

1. Cummings et al., *Arch Intern Med* 1989; 149:2445-8
2. United States Department of Health and Human Services
3. Blue Cross and Blue Shield of Texas (BCBSTX), a division of Health Care Service Corporation
4. Best, B. Making the Choice: Can Calorie Restriction Work in Humans 1998; *LEF Magazine*
5. www.healthnotes.com
6. Ody, P., *The Complete Medicinal Herbal* 1993; Dorling Kindersley
7. Tyler, VE., *Tyler's Honest Herbal* 4th Edition 1999; The Hawthorn Herbal Press
8. Murray, MT., *The Healing Power of Herbs* 2nd Edition 1995; Prima Publishing
9. Tierra, M., *Planetary Herbology* 1992; Lotus Press
10. Wren, RC., *Potter's Newcyclopaedia of Botanical Drugs & Preparations* 1988; Potter's (Herbal Supplies) Ltd.
11. Blumenthal, M., Goldberb, A., Brinckman, *J., Herbal Medicine Expanded Commission E Monographs* 2000; Integrative Medicine Communications
12. *PDR for Herbal Medicines* 1st Edition 1998; Medical Economics Company Inc.

Chapter 11

1. *National Centre for Health Statistics*; National Health Interview Survey (NHIS) 2000
2. Healthy People 2000, U.S. *Department of Health and Human Services.*
3. "Prevention of Work-Related Psychological Disorders": A National Strategy Proposed by the National Institute for Occupational Safety and Health (NIOSH), *American Psychologist*, Vol. 45, No. 10, October 1990.
4. Azar, B., *APA Monitor Online* 1999; 30:6
5. *Harvard Medical School's Consumer Health Information*; Stress and Medical Conditions
6. www.who.int/word-health-day ; Sedentary Lifestyle: A Global Public Health Problem
7. Chow R, Harrison JE, Notarius C. *Br Med J* 1987;295:1441-4
8. Salamone LM, Cauley JA, Black DM, et al. *Am J Clin Nutr* 1999;70:97-103

Index

A

additives to food, 8, 9, 28, 29
adrenaline, 121, 122, 124
aerobic exercise, 129
aging
    antioxidants, 17, 40, 41, 80, 113
    and blueberries, 79, 80
    brain, 111
    exercise, 131
    free radicals, 14, 15, 17, 40,
    41, 109
    heart, 110
    herbal remedies, 113, 116, 118,
    119
    hormone changes, 110
    immune system, 111, 112
    muscle mass, 111
    optimizing your health, 112
    protein extracts, 116, 117
    skin, 111
    supplements, 113, 117, 118,
    119
    two main theories, 109
AIDS, 15
air pollution, 6, 8, 15, 43
    and heart disease, 18

    and respiratory diseases, 8, 18
alfalfa, 70
allium compounds, 83
allyl methyl trisulfide, 83
almonds, 52
aloe vera, 68, 70
Alzheimer's disease, 43
American Health Foundation, 79
American Medical Association, 39
amino acids, 116
amylase, 104
anthocyanins, 83
antioxidants, 17, 40, 41, 43, 44, 68, 77, 78
    aging and, 17, 40, 41, 80, 113
    blueberries, 79, 80
    fruits and vegetables, 80
    grape and wine polyphenols,
    81, 82
    herbs, 68, 70, 72, 113, 116, 118
    lycopene, 78, 79
    stress and, 127
anxiety, 121, 122
aphrodisiacs, 115, 116
arthritis, 38, 41, 43
asthma, 8, 16, 41
astragalus, 67, 70, 127
auto-immune diseases, 16

avena sativa, 118

B

bee pollen, 70
beta carotene, 38, 41, 44
bioflavonoids, 40
Biosphere 2, 11, 112, 135
biotin, 48
bitter orange extract, 103
black cohosh, 114, 118
bladderwrack, 70
blood sugar levels, fibre and, 87, 88
blueberries, 79, 80, 81, 113
Body Mass Index (BMI), 94
body pollution
 diagram, 21
 effects on health, 5, 7, 8, 13, 17, 136
 fighting. *See* exercise; nutrition
 lifestyle pyramid, 29, 33, 102, 137
 sources, 5, 8, 9, 10, 15, 16, 21
 stress as, 123,124, 134
bones, 38, 53, 113
boswellia, 70
botanicals. *See* herbs
bowel movements, 86
brain, 111
bran hypothesis, 85
breast cancer, 17, 39, 75, 79
broccoli, 75, 79, 83, 84
building blocks for the body, 24, 25
Burkett, Dennis, 85

C

caffeine, 53
calcium, 52, 53, 57, 58, 113
calories, 98, 99, 100, 104, 105

daily requirements, 100, 101
restriction, 112, 117, 131, 139
and weight control, 102, 104
cancer
 blueberries and, 80
 body pollution and, 17, 29, 43, 97
 exercise, 130
 fibre and, 87, 88, 89
 fruits and vegetables, 75, 77, 79
 lycopene and, 78, 79
 obesity and, 96
 phytonutrients and, 74
 polyphenols and, 81, 82
 rates increasing, 17
 stress and, 125
 sulforaphane and, 79
 vitamin C and, 41
 vitamin E and, 43
canola oil, 25, 32
capsicum, 68, 70
car and truck exhaust, 8, 18
carcinogens, 17, 29, 43
 detoxification of, 74, 75, 79
carotenoids, 75, 83
cascara bark, 66, 70
catechins, 83
catuaba, 118
cayenne. *See* capsicum
celery seeds, 70
chaste tree berry, 118
chelation, 52
chicory, 68, 70
children, 16, 17, 18
 and obesity, 95, 96
 sedentary lifestyle, 128
Chinese pearl barley, 68, 70

cholesterol levels, 88, 129

chromium, 59

citrus aurantium, 70, 103

cleaning products, 9, 12

cleansing through loss of body fat, 11

colds and stress, 126

collagen, 42

colon cancer, 36, 39, 77, 79, 88, 130

constipation, 88

copper, 52, 59

couch grass, 70

cranberry, 118

cretinism, 52

cruciferous vegetables, cancer and, 75

D

dairy products, 32

dandelion roots, 68, 70

decoctions, 66

detoxification
       cleansing by losing fat, 11
       herbs and, 67, 68
       phytonutrients and, 74

diabetes, 43
       exercise and, 130
       fibre and, 87, 88
       fruits and vegetables vs., 77
       obesity and, 97

diallyl sulfide, 83

digestive system and herbs, 68

dong quai, 114, 118

E

electrolytes, 51

endorphins, 129

energy boosters, 68

energy system and herbs, 68

Environmental Protection Agency (U.S.), 9, 10

enzymes, 36, 51, 54, 79, 104

ephedra, 103

epimedium, 118

evening primrose oil, 113, 118

exercise, 31, 103, 117, 127, 128, 129, 133, 139
       aging, 131
       benefits, 129, 132
       cancer, 130
       diabetes, 130
       heart disease, 129
       high blood pressure, 130
       osteoporosis, 130
       psychological benefits, 130
       to reduce stress, 127, 128, 129
       weight loss, 130, 131

extract, 66

eye conditions
       macular degeneration, 42, 54, 79, 113
       and phytonutrients, 80, 83

F

fast foods, 9, 29, 95

fat tissue, toxins in, 9, 10, 11, 17, 97

fatigue, 122

fats, 26, 27, 30, 33
       sources of healthy fats, 25, 32

fenugreek, 71

fermented foods and beverages, 32

fibre, 85, 92, 138
       fibre content of common foods, 91
       health benefits, 87, 88
       recommendations for intake, 89, 90

soluble vs. insoluble, 86
fibre supplements, 92
    for weight loss, 103
"fight or flight" reaction, 121, 122, 124
fish, 19, 32, 54
flavonoids, 66, 68, 75, 83
fluoride, 52
folic acid, 36, 38, 39, 48
food additives, 8, 9, 28, 29
free radicals, 14, 15, 17, 40, 41, 109,
127
    and heart disease, 81
"French Paradox," 81
fruits and vegetables, 31, 73, 74, 75,
    76, 86, 138
    antioxidant capacity, 80
    research on benefits, 77, 82
Funk, Casimir, 35, 36

G

genes, and environmental toxins, 7
German chamomile, 68, 71
ginger root, 68, 71
ginkgo, 113, 118
ginseng, 62, 66, 67
gluco-sinolates, 84
goiter, 52
goldenseal, 114, 118
gotu kola, 118
grandiflorum, 118
grapes, 81, 82, 83
green vegetables, 31, 58, 83, 84
growth hormone, 116, 117

H

Harvard Medical School, 78
heart, and aging, 110
heart disease

body pollution and, 18
exercise, 129
fibre and, 87, 88
free radicals, 81
magnesium and, 56
obesity and, 96
stress and, 125
vitamins reducing risk, 38, 39,
    42, 44
herbal supplement, 68
herbs, 61, 72, 137, 138
    active ingredients in, 66 67
    anti-aging, 68, 113, 116, 118,
    119
    and antioxidant system, 68
    and detoxification system, 68
    and digestive system, 68
    and the drug industry, 63
    and energy system, 68
    four basic forms, 66
    herb chart, 70, 72
    history of herbal medicine, 61,
    62, 63, 65
    and immune system, 67
    increasing popularity of, 65
    medicinal qualities, 62, 63
    and prescription drugs, 64, 65,
    67
    sexual dysfunction remedies,
    115, 116
    standardization, 66, 67
    and weight loss, 103, 104
high blood pressure
    and exercise, 130
    and minerals, 58
hip fractures, 53
holistic healing, 64
Hopkins, Frederick, 36

hormones, 51, 110, 114
        changes, 110
        levels, 116
hot flashes, 114
hydrogenation, 27
hypericum, 62

I

immune system, 14, 15, 16, 64, 77
        aging, 111, 112
        amino acids and, 116
        auto-immune diseases, 16
        beta carotene and, 44
        and herbs, 62, 67
        selenium and, 55, 56
        stress and, 16, 126, 134
Industrial Revolution, 6
infertility, 55
intestinal bacteria, healthy, 32
iodine, 52, 58
iron, 38, 41, 52, 53, 58
isoflavones, 83, 115

J

Journal of the American Medical Association, 39, 55, 67
juniper berry, 71

K

kidneys, 112

L

l-arginine, 116, 119
l-glutamine, 116, 117, 118
l-lysine, 116, 119
lead contamination, 6, 42
lean meats, 32
legumes, 32, 88, 90

lemon balm, 71
licorice root, 66, 67, 68, 71, 127
lifestyle pyramid, 29, 33, 102, 137
lignans, 83
limonoids, 84
liver, 112
low-calorie diet, 112
lung cancer, 77
lupus, 16
lutein, 83
lycopene, 79, 83

M

ma huang, 103
maca, 115, 119
macular degeneration, 42, 54, 79, 113
magnesium, 52, 53, 55, 56, 58, 113
manganese, 59
marine life, 8, 13
meal replacements, 102
memory, 54, 80
menopause, 114
menstruation, 53
mercury contamination, 11
metabolism, 103, 131
milk thistle, 62, 68
mind pollution, 124
minerals, 49, 59
        calcium, 52, 53, 58
        deficiencies, 51, 52, 54, 56
        `macro' and `micro,' 51
        magnesium, 55, 56, 58
        mineral chart, 58, 59
        need for, 50, 51
        selenium, 54, 55, 57, 59
        soil depletion, 49, 50
        sources, 58, 59

supplements, 52, 54, 55, 56, 57, 137
    zinc, 54, 58
molybdenum, 59
morphine, 61
muira puama, 119
multiple sclerosis, 16
muscle mass, 111

N

National Academy of Sciences, 75, 76
National Cancer Institute, 55, 76, 86
nettle, 119
nitrates, 43
nitrites, 29, 43
nitrosamines, 43
nutrition
    23-34. *See also* fibre; fruits and vegetables; herbs; minerals; vitamins; weight control
    building blocks for the body, 24, 25
    fast food problem, 9, 29, 95
    healthy fats, 25, 26, 27, 30, 32, 33
    limiting sugar consumption, 27, 28, 33
    minimizing effects of additives, 28, 29
    whole grain products, 25, 26, 31
nuts, 32, 73, 90

O

oat fibre, 87
obesity, 93, 105, 138, 139
    Body Mass Index (BMI), 94
    and cancer, 96
    in children, 95, 96
    and diabetes, 97
    and heart disease, 96
    prevalence of, 93, 95
    reasons for, 97, 99
    weight control, 99, 104
oils for cooking, 25, 26, 27, 32
Okinawa (region in Japan), 19, 135
olive oil, 25, 32
olives, 78, 79
omega-3 fatty acids, 32
ORAC value of fruits and vegetables, 80
oral contraceptives, 39
osteoporosis, 38, 53
    fighting with exercise, 130

P

panax ginseng, 119
pantothenic acid, 48
parsley, 71
passion flower, 71
Pen Tsao, 61
pesticides, 5, 12
phaseolus vulgaris, 71
phytoestrogens, 83, 114
phytonutrients, 73, 84, 127
    benefits of, 74, 75, 76, 82
    blueberries, 79, 80, 81
    chart, 83, 84
    detoxification, 74
    grape skin polyphenols, 81, 82
    lycopene, 79
    sulforaphane, 79
    supplements, 82
pipsissewa, 71
polychlorinated biphenyls (PCBs), 8
polyphenols, 81

positive attitude, 133

potassium, 58

potatoes, 42

poultry, 32

pre-menstrual syndrome, 56

pregnant women, 39

premature deaths, 18

prescription drugs, 43

     and herbs, 64, 65, 67

preservatives, 29

preventive medicine, 63

prostate cancer, 55, 78

protein, 32

     and minerals, 52, 57

protein extracts, 116, 117

psychological benefits of exercise, 130

pygeum africanum, 119

Q

quercetins, 83

R

Recommended Dietary Allowances (RDA), 37

recycling, 12

red clover, 115, 119

red raspberry, 119

reishi mushroom, 67, 68, 71, 127

respiratory diseases and air pollution, 8, 18

resveratrol, 81, 82, 83

rheumatoid arthritis, 16, 43

rose hips, 68, 71

roughage, 87, 88

S

salicyn, 64

sarsaparilla, 71

saturated fats, 27

schisandra berry, 68, 72

sedentary lifestyle, 97, 99, 127, 128

selenium, 52, 54, 55, 57, 59, 75

sexual dysfunction, herbal remedies, 115, 116

Siberian ginseng, 67, 68, 72

skin, 111

smaller meals, 100

smoking, 42

soft drinks, 28, 29, 33, 99

soil depletion, 49, 50

soy, 83, 114

St. John's Wort, 62

standardization for herbs, 66, 67

stress

     as body pollution, 123, 124, 134

     cancer, 125

     colds, 126

     from environment, 121, 122, 123

     exercise for, 127, 128, 129

     "fight or flight" reaction, 121, 122, 124

     heart disease, 125

     immune system, 126, 134

     impact on health, 125, 126

     nutrition and, 127

     reduction, 126, 127, 139

     types, 122

sugars, 27, 28, 33, 98, 99

sulforaphane, 79, 84

supplements, 31, 33, 39, 40, 44, 137, 139

     aging, 113, 117, 118, 119

     fibre, 92, 103

     herbal, 68, 69

synergy, 64, 75

T

tamarind, 72
teas, 66
thyme, 72
tinctures, 66
tomatoes, 78, 79, 83
tonics, 68
toxic substances
     5. *See also* body pollution
     cleaning body of. *See*
     detoxification, free radicals, 14,
     15, 17, 40, 41, 109, 127
     sources of, 10, 21
trans fats, 27
transportation, air pollution from, 8, 18
tribulus, 116, 119
turmeric, 72

U

University of Toronto, 79
unsaturated fats, 26, 27
urinary tract infections, 80
uva ursi, 72

V

vitamin A, 24, 37, 46
vitamin B1 (thiamin), 35, 47
vitamin B2 (riboflavin), 47
vitamin B3 (niacin), 47
vitamin B6, 38, 39, 47
vitamin B12, 38, 39, 47
vitamin C, 29, 35, 38, 41, 43, 46, 113
vitamin D, 37, 38, 46, 53, 113
vitamin E, 37, 38, 43, 44, 46, 52, 55, 57, 113
vitamin K, 37, 46
vitamins, 35, 45, 127
     supplements, 39, 40, 44, 137
     `synthetic' and `natural,' 40
     vitamin chart, 46, 48
     water-soluble and fat-soluble, 37

W

washing fruit and vegetables, 10
water
     importance for body, 31, 34
     pollution, 6, 8
working with fibre, 91
weight-bearing exercises, 139
weight control, 99, 104
     exercise, 130, 131
weight training, 131
whales, 8
white blood cells, 16, 55, 62
white flour, 25, 26
white kidney bean extract, 104
white meats, 95
white willow bark, 64, 65
whole grain products, 25, 26, 31, 90
wine, 81
World Health Organization, 65, 93, 96

Y

yerba mate, 72

Z

zeaxanthin, 83
zinc, 52, 54, 58, 113, 127